GOURMET
VEGETABLES

Smart Tips and Tasty Picks for
Gardeners and Gourmet Cooks

Anne Raver-Editor

FOR THE
ADVANCE
MENT OF
BOTANY
AND THE
SERVICE OF
THE CITY

BROOKLYN
BOTANIC
GARDEN
PUBLICATIONS
·MMII·

Janet Marinelli
SERIES EDITOR

Sigrun Wolff Saphire
ASSOCIATE EDITOR

Mark Tebbitt
SCIENCE EDITOR

Anne Garland
ART DIRECTOR

Steven Clemants
VICE-PRESIDENT, SCIENCE & PUBLICATIONS

Judith D. Zuk
PRESIDENT

Elizabeth Scholtz
DIRECTOR EMERITUS

Handbook #171
Copyright © 2002 by Brooklyn Botanic Garden, Inc.
Handbooks in the *21st-Century Gardening Series,* formerly *Plants & Gardens,*
are published quarterly at 1000 Washington Ave., Brooklyn, NY 11225.
Subscription included in Brooklyn Botanic Garden subscriber membership dues ($35.00 per year).
ISBN # 1-889538-51-5
Printed by Science Press, a division of the Mack Printing Group.
Printed on recycled paper.

TABLE OF CONTENTS

FRESH FROM THE GARDEN

ANNE RAVER

WHAT IS A GOURMET VEGETABLE, ANYWAY? Something you've never heard of? Something crucial to Thai cooking? A baby something, as in baby carrot, baby corn? Something that looks as if it grows at the bottom of the ocean? I have pored over glossy food magazines, gorgeous garden cookbooks, the essays of favorite food and garden writers. The only answer I've come up with is this: something exquisitely fresh and delectable.

Now, that could be good old 'Silver Queen' corn, which is leagues ahead of that awful super-sweet stuff that tastes like white sugar and is promoted by an industry mostly interested in long shelf life. 'Silver Queen', of course, must be ripped off the stalk while the pot is on the boil. But what a wonderful ritual! It only adds to the special feeling of the occasion. The 'Silver Queen' is ripe!

The same thing holds for a truly delicious tomato. I have not found a modern hybrid to match the complex, softly acid flavors of an heirloom tomato like 'Brandywine' or 'Prudens Purple', blending together in the back of my throat like a fine wine.

Peas are another example. Who could sniff at a mess of perfectly picked 'Lincoln' peas, steamed and smothered in butter, and say, "How boring"? The joy of savoring that old-time pea has led me to edamame, the fresh soybean pods so beloved in Japan and popularized here by Japanese restaurants. Over time, they found their way into the seed catalogs.

Gourmet vegetables may lead the adventurous gardener on a quest, like the one the food historian William Woys Weaver set out on when he began to re-create unique strains of Native American corn by growing out seed, selecting the most promising ears, then growing that seed, and on back down the line until a plant resembling the original configuration, of say, a speckled corn like 'Bear Dance', with its violet, purple, blue, gray, and cream kernels, flourished in his garden. Weaver also makes green tortillas from the cornmeal he grinds from a dent corn called 'Oaxacan Green'.

Who can eat 'Yellow Bantam' after this? (Well, I can.) A gourmet vegetable is whatever speaks to your personal palate, your sense of the memorable, that moment

Opposite: An array of freshly picked summer vegetables ready for the gourmet chef.

Cabbage, kale, and collards get a visual boost from flowering plants, such as coleus and cannas above.

of biting into something you may never experience, just that way, ever again.

I think a quiet revolution has been under way among American food lovers. Maybe it started with the realization that we didn't have to eat tennis-ball tomatoes in the winter. We could simply stop eating tomatoes—until they ripened once again in our gardens. Or we could eat them in sauces made from the ones we picked fresh last summer or froze from a bushel bought at a favorite farm stand.

Our gardens have grown more international, with tomatillos spilling into the tomato patch, accompanied by cilantro and chiles for salsa. We grow eggplants and big poblano peppers to roast over a homemade grill; we learn how to cook long, graceful okra pods in spicy Indian dishes that cry out for fenugreek. Fenugreek? What's fenugreek? And where do you find it? Not on the shelves of most grocery stores, that's for sure. The toothed grassy herb, native to southern Europe, makes an excellent green manure, and its tangy young shoots are key to the unforgettable flavor of okra and green mangos in Indian dishes.

A gourmet vegetable is more vigorous, more delicious grown in organic soil teeming with earthworms and microorganisms. (If you don't believe me, try it yourself.) A gourmet vegetable looks better grown with flowers and herbs; a bowl of greens tastes better with peppery orange nasturtiums sprinkled on top.

We get so addicted to these flavors, we start pushing the limits of our designated "zones" with cold frames and row covers and hoop houses. We sprout lentils and mung beans in old Mason jars to brighten a February salad. We dig root cellars to keep all those heirloom potatoes through the long, dark winter.

Maybe a gourmet vegetable is more a frame of mind than it is any one species or variety. It is certainly one I like to eat—fresh and perfectly cooked and eaten with good friends and a glass of wine.

THE REWARDS OF REGIONALLY GROWN FOODS

GARY PAUL NABHAN

WHEN YOU SIT DOWN AT YOUR DINNER TABLE and look at the food you've placed before your friends or family, do you ever consider how much of it has been grown at a place that you've actually visited? Have you had a chance to observe how it's been grown, how healthy the soil feels, how much wildlife thrives around the edges of the garden, and how the harvesters feel about their work? Thinking about questions such as these can influence which foods you purchase to supplement what you grow at home, and, just as important, who and where you buy it from. Many folks are

One way to enjoy the seasonal bounty of locally grown foods is to buy fresh fruit and vegetables at a farmers' market.

Top: Ever wonder what's been sprayed on your food? By buying from a local organic farmer, you can be sure the food is raised in an environmentally sound way. Bottom: Small-scale organic farming promotes the well-being of local wildlife, including this American toad.

obtaining an ever-increasing portion of their food directly from those who grow it—for example, by way of community-supported agriculture projects, local farm stands, or farmers' markets. By choosing to buy from known sources, they can be sure that the food was raised in a way that keeps the land, as well as those who work and live on it, healthy.

Such choices fly in the face of national trends: Most of the food consumed in North America today travels an average of 1,500 miles before it lands on a plate. That is 22 percent farther than food had to travel in 1981. In light of our own food security, it is perhaps more disturbing to note that the amount of produce eaten by people in the United States but grown on other continents has doubled since 1980, to nearly 22 percent of all the produce eaten in the U.S.

Ironically, at least 10 percent of the foods that are now hauled to us over long distances could be obtained from farms within 50 miles of

8

Participants in community-supported agriculture projects purchase a share in the harvest of a local farm at the start of the year and receive seasonal fruits and vegetables as they become available throughout the growing season.

where we live. Growing even that much of our diet locally could save hundreds of millions of gallons of fossil fuel that are now used to ship half a million truckloads of fruit and vegetables across the American continent each year. It would not only save energy but also drastically reduce carbon dioxide emissions.

Beyond the environmental and economic benefits, the rewards of eating more locally grown food can be seen, smelled, tasted, and last but not least, assimilated by our bodies: Locally grown foods are fresher, more nutritious, and keep us connected to our surroundings. The seasonal pulses of ripening fruits and vegetables increase our awareness of our local environment, making each harvest time special. You simply don't feel that connection when purchasing strawberries grown someplace in the Southern Hemisphere during the middle of our winter. And, naturally, when shopping locally, you can also enjoy conversations with the farmers, fishermen, and orchard keepers in your area and support their efforts to keep family businesses afloat.

Rather than assuming that the global marketplace should give us whatever food we may fancy at any time of the year, we can tune in to the unique local bounty of the moment. Of course, not all vegetables grow equally well in all climates. But the commitment to eating locally grown food—as I have done for 80 percent of my foodstuffs over the past few years—has made me more aware of local heirloom vegetables, unique fruit varieties, and regionally produced milk and cheeses from minor breeds of sheep and goats that forage on native plants. The more locally grown food I eat, the deeper I know the land, the weather, and the agricultural history of my region. And the more my senses marvel at the fragrances and flavors of my home ground.

GROWING THE WINTER HARVEST

ELIOT COLEMAN AND BARBARA DAMROSCH

MODERN SUPERMARKETS OFFER SHOPPERS the false luxury of buying any food, from anywhere in the world, at any time. True luxury is being able to choose what is close at hand, picked when it is fresh, ripe, perfect, safe, and full of the power to impart health. Since this is the way we like to eat, we figured out how to do it on the coast of Maine, every day of the year. For six years we have run a "backwards" farm, where we market fresh produce in a season that begins in October and runs through May. So that the word "fresh" really means something, our produce is never sold more than 25 miles from where it was grown.

Our system is a simple one that runs on three basic principles. The first is *cold-hardy vegetables*—ones that tolerate below-freezing or near-freezing temperatures. The second principle is *succession planting*—sowing the crops at close intervals from late summer through late fall to keep the cornucopia coming right through

With some protection many vegetables, such as the radishes above, can be grown right through cold northern winters, extending the growing season to year-round.

the winter. The third is *protected cultivation*. In nature, hardy vegetables frequently survive under a blanket of snow. We've found that the gardener can blanket them reliably and economically with cold frames or with plastic greenhouses made doubly efficient by adding an inner protective layer suspended about a foot above the crops. In doing this, we are not so much extending the growing season—which requires expensive heating and lighting—as we are extending the harvest season by merely keeping the plants alive and healthy. A friend once compared our system to a giant crisper

Planted in early fall, these crops will soon be protected against the coming winter cold by a mobile greenhouse. In the colder months, gardeners don't have to worry about weeding, watering, or pests.

drawer in the fridge from which you can continually pluck your supper.

We have tested many vegetables to see which work best in a winter growing system, and a large number are salad crops. Perhaps you've noticed how spinach can yield all winter if shielded from snow and ice. Mâche (also known as corn salad), with its tiny, mild-tasting rosettes, is equally valiant. Leaves from beet varieties such as the crimson 'Bulls Blood' or the red-veined 'Red Ace' look beautiful in salads when picked at three inches high. Claytonia (miner's lettuce), with little heart-shaped leaves on slender stems, is also super hardy. Others that we grow all season with a bit of midwinter heat include lettuces like 'Samantha', 'Galactic', and 'Tango'; peppery arugula; minutina (buck's horn plantain, erba stella), with its slender antler-shaped leaves; narrow-stemmed chard; watercress; and frisée endive—a gorgeously frilled golden variety called 'Bianca Riccia'. We've tried dozens of Asian greens; winners include tatsoi, mizuna, pak choi, red mustard, komatsuna, pak choi 'Autumn Poem', and the beautiful yel-

Grown as a cut-and-come-again crop, the crimson leaves of 'Bull's Blood', a beet variety, can be harvested throughout the winter, making a tasty addition to salads.

low, loose-leafed Chinese cabbages such as 'Tokyo Bekana'. All the greens except mâche are grown as cut-and-come-again crops, harvested at "baby leaf" size. Not only are they more tender and delicious at this stage, but they also withstand the cold better than at full-head size and regrow more vigorously after cutting than they would from new sowings.

We've also succeeded with leeks, Swiss chard, broccoli raab, scallions, chicory, dandelions, escarole, garlic greens, kale, kohlrabi, collards, parsley, peas, radicchio, and sorrel. And while we grow some root crops for storage, we have been delighted at how much tastier they are when fresh-dug in winter. 'Napoli' carrots, wildly popular because of their extra-sweet taste, are the stars of the show, along with radishes and wonderful little sweet, white 'Hakurei' turnips, which we harvest at golf-ball size. Their greens are delicious too.

The succession-planting routine is something we have worked out over the years—it takes some tinkering to figure maturity dates for specific crops in winter's uncharted territory. They grow more slowly and must make most of their growth in fall, before the day length drops below ten hours. The later the planting, the longer the crop takes to reach harvest size. Most of our sowing takes place from mid-August through fall, but we keep planting right through the winter to replace spent crops and to ensure that we have plenty coming along for spring.

When we first experimented with this system as home gardeners, we relied on cold frames, which we covered with a simple 32-foot-long mobile plastic greenhouse, easily built at a cost of $2 per square foot. We found that each layer of protection moved the garden a zone and a half to the south. By combining the

Minutina, or buck's horn plantain, so named for its slender, antler-shaped leaves, is one of the many salad greens suitable for winter culture.

two, we gave the crops a Zone 8 winter, like Georgia's, instead of the Zone 5 winter we experience in Maine. We now have a series of 100-foot by 30-foot plastic-covered greenhouses—some mobile, some not; some unheated, some heated to just above freezing to take the chilly edge off January and February for the crops that need it. Instead of cold frames we use a blanket of spun-bonded polyester fabric (a brand such as Remay), held a foot above the crops on wire wickets inside the greenhouses. It is inexpensive, does not require venting, lets in enough light for good growth, and offers almost as much protection as the cold frames did, so we now use it in our small home greenhouse as well.

Other growing practices are simple, too. In the cold months there is no weeding to do, no watering, and, except for the odd vole, no pests. Our soil-fertility program is compost-based, on the theory that what nature puts into organic matter is a complete package of nutrients, and that crops fed this diet will give us a complete nutritional package in return.

When we tell people we eat homegrown vegetables all winter, they are skeptical. Americans tend to write off winter as a sort of culinary and horticultural Antarctica, unaware that many crops perform better when the air is crisp. All it takes is one taste to change their minds. The carrots have crunch, the spinach is full of life. And week-old greens on the supermarket shelf can't compare with the freshness and quality of those that go from soil to salad bowl on the same blustery day.

To find out more about the winter harvest, see "For More Information," page 103.

EXPERIMENTING WITH ANCIENT CROPS

ANNE RAVER

ABOUT EIGHT YEARS AGO, my sister, Martha, and I pulled an all-nighter trying to unlock the secrets of amaranth grain, the ancient Aztec crop. We tried it popped and in porridge and pancakes. But all we ended up with was high-protein grit.

We tried to grind the amaranth seeds into flour in the food processor, but the blades couldn't chop the tiny black grains, as small as poppy seeds. The coffee grinder didn't work either. No wonder the Aztecs used rocks—a mortar and pestle made from stone—to crush these seeds into flour.

Amaranth (*Amaranthus* species) is so beautiful, I don't care if I never figure out how to eat it, though it would be nice. My first variety, 'Warihio', grew to a ten-foot, reddish-green stalk with a purplish-red plume as curvy as an elephant's trunk and as fluffy as a feather duster. Hidden inside the red plumes' florets were

Quinoa, an ancient American grain, is high in protein and has a lightly nutty taste.

In Central and South America, amaranth has been a food source for about 10,000 years.

thousands of tiny black seeds full of protein and lysine, an essential amino acid lacking in many other grains. When amaranth is combined with other grains, such as corn—as was the Aztec custom—the resulting protein contains most of the amino acids essential to human health.

The grain, which has been grown for about 10,000 years in Central and South America, was so revered by the Aztecs that they mixed the seeds with blood to make little figures of their gods, to be eaten during religious ceremonies. When the conquistadors arrived in Mexico in the 16th century, they saw the sacrament as a mockery of their own practice of Holy Communion. Thereafter, anyone caught with the grain was condemned to death—a fairly effective way to stamp out a religion—and the crop went underground, along with many of its devotees.

In his book *Coming Home to Eat* (W.W. Norton, 2001), Gary Paul Nabhan points out that the Sonoran Indians used to get down on their hands and knees and graze on wild amaranth when its young leaves first emerged in the desert. The Spanish missionaries who observed them, he writes, "would not stoop to this same ecstatic pursuit." Instead, they condemned the Indians as "little more than wild animals." The missionaries had apparently forgotten, as Nabhan points out, that their own ancestors—the early monastics in the Middle East—had also foraged on their hands and knees, literally following "Christ's instruction to imitate the birds of the air and herds of the field."

Not so in the Sonoran Desert, where the Christians quickly suppressed the herb. But Nabhan harks back to the practice, gathering wild greens like amaranth, lamb's quarters, and purslane when they spring up with the summer rains. The Sonorans call them *quelites de las aguas,* "the wild spinaches of the summer rains." Nabhan's recipe sounds pretty good to me. He sautés a few scallions and poblano chiles, then adds a mound of hand-washed greens to the saucepan. As soon as the leaves wilt, he eats them. "Their flavors were so fresh, so buzzed with their recent photosynthetic surge," he writes, that within "min-

By the time its grain ripens, amaranth is quite tall.
In the spring, many varieties produce tasty leaves.

utes of devouring them, I felt more green, as if I were on some folic acid high."

But to get back to amaranth, harvesting its seeds was quite an adventure. I cut the plumes off the stalks and dried them for about five days on a sheet spread out on the sunny cement terrace. (If it rains, you run out and cover them up with a tarp or something, which we did with limited success.) Then you stomp on the plumes (with clean feet) or rub them over a screen to release the seeds, and pretty soon you have a few small hills of amaranth grain. The seeds are covered with pink chaff—the remains of the amaranth flowers—but when they are poured from one big pot to another outdoors in the face of a breeze, most of the chaff flies off, leaving pretty clean seeds.

We carried our offering into the kitchen, where we bumbled about in our ignorance. First we tried to pop it, dry, in an iron skillet, as suggested by the Seeds of Change catalog. But when we shook the pan, the little grains didn't roll about as easily as popcorn does, and they started to burn. I took the lid off and stirred them with a wooden spoon, but then the seeds—which were popping into the teensiest of white balls—popped right out of the pan. I tried adding a little butter. In the end, they weren't bad—if you like grit with scorched butter—with a slightly nutty-sweet taste. Then we tried tossing a few handfuls into regular pancake batter, figuring that maybe the heat from the skillet would release the flavor of the amaranth. No such luck. The pancakes weren't bad with lots of real maple syrup, but you couldn't taste the seeds. The porridge wasn't any better. I dumped a whole cup of seeds into two cups of boiling water, and let it cook slowly, to the consistency of grits. It tasted a bit like rhubarb, but by then we might have been hallucinating.

A few weeks later, a friend informed me that I had grown the wrong kind of amaranth: "The golden varieties are best for grain." So, this year I'm going to try again, with 'Golden Giant', whose young leaves are also supposed to be good eaten raw or steamed. I have since read that a Sonoran variety, 'Mayo', which is an intense purple-red, is good for eating, and that a variety called 'Red Leaf Vegetable'

16

has green and burgundy coleus-like leaves that are good cooked or in salads. The best way to rediscover the pleasures of eating an ancient crop is to talk to people whose ancestors handed down the secrets to them. Native Seed/SEARCH, in Tucson, Arizona, is one good place to start. Its catalog lists a dozen amaranth varieties, so people there are well versed in its culinary secrets. The golden or tan varieties are most often used as a cooked grain or for popping; the red varieties are used for their leaves or to make dye. To cook the grain, pour one cup of amaranth seeds into three cups of water, bring to a boil, then simmer for 25 minutes. To make flour, roast the seeds in the oven for 45 minutes at 325°F, stirring occasionally. Then put the seeds in a hand mill or blender. It's best to mix amaranth flour with another grain flour, as the amaranth has no gluten. To pop the grain, put one tablespoon of seeds into an ungreased wok or deep cast-iron skillet over medium heat and simply move the grains constantly with a brush until they pop.

Quinoa (*Chenopodium quinoa*) is another ancient high-protein grain with a lightly nutty taste. I intend to give it a whirl this summer as well. One of my favorite seed sources, J.L. Hudson, offers three varieties: 'Cherry Vanilla', whose seed heads are creamy white to rose; 'Orange Head', with vivid orange seed heads, and 'Rainbow', with multicolored seed heads. Hudson also offers the intriguing ancient Mexican vegetable Huazontle (*Chenopodium nuttalliae*), which produces mild, spinachlike leaves and seeds that can be ground into a delicious meal. Devil's claw (*Proboscidea louisianica*), cultivated by Southwestern tribes, produces seed rich in oil and protein, and the black fiber of the fruit or "claw" is used for weaving baskets. The young fruits are cooked as an okra-like vegetable, and the dried seeds, pried out with a kind of blunt needle or a pair of pliers, may be peeled and eaten. The sprawling plants produce sweet-smelling lavender flowers.

The Incas grew ocha, or oca (*Oxalis tuberosa*)—which is now coming back to American gardens—for its edible tubers more than a thousand years ago. In *Heirloom Vegetable Gardening* (Henry Holt, 1997), William Woys Weaver tells how the tubers were sent from Peru to England in 1829, where they "immediately caused a gardening sensation." Oca blanca (white-rooted) and oca colorada (red-rooted) are two ocha varieties, producing tubers of a shape similar to those of Jerusalem artichokes, but with waxy skins and brilliant colors. Weaver starts these in pots in late winter and plants them in the garden when all danger of frost is past. He eats the greens as a vegetable, but if he wants to harvest the tubers later in the season, he leaves the tops alone.

Oxalis thrives in cool weather and does best, Weaver has discovered, in partial shade. *Oxalis tetraphylla* (*O. deppei*), known as lucky clover due to its shamrocklike leaves, was introduced from Mexico in 1837. The plants need sandy soil to produce carrotlike roots about three inches long. Weaver says they have a delicate flavor, but that you must allow them to "mellow in the sun for several days to remove the bitterness." He also enjoys the shamrock-shaped leaves and pink flowers in salads.

Growing such crops not only brings new flavors and textures to the table, it opens a window to another time and culture. And when I see those plumes of tall amaranth dangling in my garden, I feel a little closer to the people who knew its secrets so many thousands of years ago.

ENCYCLOPEDIA
OF GOURMET
VEGETABLES

On the following pages are detailed portraits of the authors' favorite vegetables, organized in alphabetical order by common name. Browse through this section to discover the tastiest vegetable varieties and find out how to grow them in your garden. Most varieties are accompanied by a number indicating the days to maturity, which gives you an idea how long it takes from starting seed or transplanting to harvesting the mature vegetable. All year long the seasonal pickings can inspire your culinary adventures.

For information on plant hardiness, consult the USDA hardiness zone map on page 102.

ARTICHOKES
Cynara scolymus
HENRY N. HOMEYER

California lays claim to every single artichoke that's produced commercially in the United States and Canada, and industry promoters would like you to think that you must live in California to grow them. Don't believe it. I grow and consume at least half a dozen artichokes every year in New Hampshire, sometimes twice that number. Not only do they taste great, but they also look gorgeous in the flower garden; be forewarned that their striking gray-green foliage may cause the neighbors to stop and ask what on earth you are growing.

Raising artichokes does take a little extra work, but almost anyone can do it. Artichokes generally produce their flower buds, which is what we eat, in the second year of their existence. In places like Monterey County, California, the plants are perennials and produce edible buds for several years. But in colder areas, where the plants cannot survive the winter outdoors, you need to play a little three-card monte with your artichokes, convincing them that they have gone through a winter by the time you plant them outdoors in their first year.

Whether steamed, boiled, or baked, artichokes are easy to prepare and taste great served with melted butter, mayonnaise, or a dipping sauce.

GROWING ARTICHOKES

Start artichoke seeds indoors in February. They will germinate in ten days or more at 70°F to 75°F. Once they have germinated, keep the seedlings at 65°F to 70°F for about six weeks. Set up fluorescent lights six to eight inches above the plants, and provide them with artificial light for 14 hours each day. (By the way, you don't need to buy fancy grow-lights; any fluorescent bulb will work.)

Ideally, night temperatures should dip to about 55°F to 60°F. Just turning off the lights will cool the air somewhat, but, if it's still too warm, crack open a window. Once the first set of true leaves are three inches long, transplant the seedlings to four-inch pots.

Now comes the tricky part—simulating winter. You can do this by taking the seedlings to a place where

Stunning in the flower garden, artichoke plants grow quite large and require a lot of space.

temperatures hover between 40°F and 50°F. I grow mine under lights in the basement, which is naturally cold in early spring. If you don't have a suitable place indoors, move the seedlings to a sheltered spot outdoors. Ideally, they should spend two weeks in an environment where temperatures never climb above 50°F. If the weather report indicates a heat wave or a cold snap, move the pots of artichokes into the house or garage. Artichokes will survive temperatures in the low 20s, though young plants are not as tough as mature ones. (And if you can't manage to give them a cool period in the spring, plant artichokes anyway. I know gardeners in the north of the country who get artichokes each year without any tricks.)

When the soil temperature reaches 50°F, plant the artichokes in a spot in the garden where they get at least six hours of sunshine per day. They are big plants and should be spaced about two feet apart for best results. They are not too fussy, but they are heavy feeders and like moist, well-drained soil. Prepare the soil accordingly by adding compost and one cup of granular organic fertil-

TUNISIAN DIPPING SAUCE

3 tbsp. olive oil
$^1/_4$ cup lemon juice
$^1/_2$ cup fresh cilantro (coriander leaf), chopped
3 large cloves garlic, crushed
1 tbsp. gourmet rice wine vinegar
Salt and pepper to taste

Mix all the ingredients in a bowl and serve. Makes enough dipping sauce for four to six artichokes.

izer per plant. (Organic fertilizers are better for many reasons; their ability to release nutrients slowly to the plants is an important one.) Artichokes need almost neutral or slightly sweet soil; a pH of 6.5 to 8.0 works best.

Commercial artichokes are given heavy doses of fertilizer and are irrigated daily. Homegrown artichokes will do best if you never let the soil dry out completely. Minimize watering needs during dry spells by mulching around the plants with straw or leaves.

Artichokes grow best in fairly cool weather, which is why they thrive on the coast of California. They will sulk a bit in the heat of August but become productive in the fall. Each plant will produce one big artichoke and two to six smaller ones from side shoots. Harvest the artichokes before the buds open, or they will be tough.

RECOMMENDED VARIETIES

Days to maturity listed below are counted from the time of transplanting.

'GREEN GLOBE'—85 days; the standard for many years; sweet and tasty.

'IMPERIAL STAR'—85 to 95 days; hybrid; claimed to produce more artichokes than 'Green Globe', not much difference in practice; sweet and tasty.

EATING ARTICHOKES

Steam or boil the artichokes until you can easily pull off an outside leaf (or bract, to be botanically accurate). Depending on the size of the artichoke, this may take from 10 to 30 minutes. Serve with melted butter or mayonnaise. Both are good for dipping, as is Tunisian dipping sauce (see recipe on this page), a low-calorie alternative.

Another approach to preparing artichokes is even simpler. Trim the tips of the leaves and level the bases of the artichokes, then place them in a pot. Drizzle each one with a little olive oil, sprinkle with *herbes de Provence,* and place a slice of lemon on top. Add water until the artichokes are sitting in liquid up to their hips, or about one-third of the way up; add a tablespoon of the herb blend to the water, cover the pot, and cook until done. No sauce is necessary.

As for me, I love eating artichokes fresh from the garden—and being the only one on my block to do so.

ASPARAGUS
Asparagus officinalis
CAROLE SAVILLE

When I eat asparagus, I always think of my neighbor, Mr. Tunis—volunteer fireman, school bus driver, jolly good fellow, and generous gardener—who stopped by one spring day in his red pickup truck and brought me an armful of asparagus crowns from his abundant garden. I was a rank beginner, digging my first garden in the shelter of the stone walls left from an old dairy barn in rural New Jersey. As an enthusiastic novice, I attributed my flourishing asparagus patch, which improved with every year, to the things I learned from the vegetable books I studiously read. In reality, my thriving plantation of asparagus probably owed a lot more to those thick stone walls, which warmed the elegant, green spears grown at their base.

Aside from the pleasure of harvesting your own, you get to watch the spears not cut for the table grow into delicate foliage plants with billowing ferny branches that may reach five feet in height. They make a handsome backdrop for a flower border and also look good planted sentry-style along a walkway. The female plants produce vivid red berries; the male plants do not. Though the female plants produce thicker spears, the male plants produce a larger number of them, since they don't have to expend their energy making fruit. These days, many gardeners are planting only the all-male or predominantly male hybrids, such as 'Jersey Giant' or 'UC 157', for a greater yield.

Asparagus, a winter-dormant, herbaceous perennial, grows well in most North American climate zones, with the exception of the coldest, the warmest, and the most humid areas. Traditionally, the "quickest" route to harvesting your own asparagus is to plant bare-root crowns

Starting an asparagus patch requires a bit of work intially, but it will stay productive for many years.

in deep trenches, which will net you a small number of spears in the second year, followed by sizeable harvests after the third year. You can also start asparagus from seed, with a small harvest the third year and a full harvest in the fourth and each following year. Generally, gardeners purchase seed only of those varieties for which crowns are not available, such as the heirloom 'Argenteuil', a savory French asparagus with thick, handsome rosy-purple and green stalks.

GROWING ASPARAGUS

Diligence in the preparation of asparagus beds—and patience—are the initial requirements for enjoying harvests of the vegetable over many seasons to come. A heavy feeder, asparagus requires soil with a pH of 6.5 to 7 that is rich in organic matter and provides excellent drainage. As the asparagus beds can remain productive for ten years or more in the same place, it's vital to dig the patch deeply when you start. In early spring, choose a site in full sun and turn over the soil, removing all weeds and grass. Amend the soil with compost or well-aged manure, and add one pound of bonemeal or two pounds of rock phosphate for every 25 feet of row.

How much asparagus should you plant? The rule of thumb is that 30 to 40 crowns will suit a family of four. To prepare beds for that quantity, dig two trenches six to eight inches deep (or one foot deep in cold areas) and one foot wide, approximately 20 feet long, and three to four feet apart. Plant the crowns 15 inches apart, spreading their roots out in a circular fashion over a small mound of soil. Cover them with several inches of soil. As the shoots gradually break through the surface, keep filling the trench with soil until it reaches ground level, then spread four to six inches of an organic mulch, like salt hay, cocoa hulls, or fir or oak leaves, to help eliminate weeds, provide extra nutrients, and conserve moisture. The asparagus patch needs to be watered well during its first year but will require only moderate amounts of water during the following growing seasons. When the long-awaited day of the asparagus harvest arrives, cut six- to eight-inch spears on an angle just below the soil level and savor the rewards of your labor. Once the asparagus crowns are full-grown, the harvest season will last about six to eight weeks every year.

Rust and *Cercospora* leaf spot are diseases that plague asparagus, and the best approach is to plant varieties that have proven disease-resistant. Rust is associated with damp weather conditions, and *Cercospora* can invade asparagus in the Southeast. Consult a local nursery or your cooperative extension about which asparagus varieties are best adapted to your USDA zone. The asparagus beetle is a prevalent pest, but covering beds at planting time with floating row covers is an effective deterrent. If the beds are already infested, conduct a diligent fall cleanup, followed in early spring by hand-picking of the beetles, their larvae, and their eggs.

Opposite: Once the asparagus crowns are full-grown, they will produce fresh spears, such as these purple ones, for about six to eight weeks every year.

With the exception of 'Argenteuil', an heirloom variety that needs to be started from seed, all the varieties mentioned in the following list are available as crowns.

'ARGENTEUIL'—French heirloom; grown from seed; thick, rose-purple and whitish-green spears with excellent flavor. Traditional variety for blanching (white asparagus).

'JERSEY GIANT'—Productive all-male hybrid; large succulent green spears with purple-tinted bracts; tolerant of rust, *Fusarium* wilt, and crown rot; good for colder climates.

'JERSEY KING'—Predominantly male hybrid, exceptionally large, tender spears with tight, round purplish bracts; widely adapted and resistant to rust, *Fusarium* wilt, and crown and root rot.

'JERSEY KNIGHT'—Vigorous all-male hybrid with large, bright green spears with purple tips; consistently high yields; widely adapted and highly resistant to rust, and tolerant of *Fusarium* wilt as well as crown and root rot; excellent disease resistance among the all-male hybrids.

'MARY WASHINGTON'—Heirloom; produces husky, straight, dark green spears with purple tinge on tightly folded tips; also good for canning or freezing; rust-resistant.

'PURPLE PASSION'—Predominantly male hybrid; a European favorite with deep garnet, medium-size spears; very sweet and stringless; decorative in the garden but fades to green when cooked; however, the pretty purple slim young spears can be eaten raw or used as a garnish.

'UC 157'—Predominantly male hybrid; commercial variety developed for mild-winter areas of the Pacific coast, the Southwest, and the South; vigorous producer with large green spears of superb flavor; resistant to rust and tolerant of *Fusarium* wilt.

ASPARAGUS IN VINAIGRETTE

1/2 pound pencil-thin asparagus per person
2 tbsp. white champagne vinegar
3 tbsp. walnut oil
3 tbsp. grape seed oil
1 tbsp. finely chopped dill
Sea salt and freshly ground black pepper to taste

Bend each asparagus spear gently, snapping off and discarding the tough ends. Steam the asparagus until just tender, about five to eight minutes. Plunge into a bowl of ice water, then drain and pat dry. Prepare the vinaigrette by whisking together all the ingredients, tasting to correct seasoning. Coat the asparagus with the vinaigrette and serve immediately.

EATING ASPARAGUS

Asparagus is an ancient vegetable, first cultivated by the Romans and used in such curious recipes as puréed asparagus tips simmered in white wine with onion, lovage, coriander, and savory, then thickened with egg yolks. If you don't want to go to all that trouble, fresh asparagus tastes fabulous briefly steamed and served with melted butter or as a salad with a vinaigrette drizzled over the vibrant green spears.

BEANS
Phaseolus vulgaris
LYNETTE L. WALTHER

Phaseolus vulgaris has been a staple in Peru and Mexico for thousands of years. It was later brought north, and Native Americans made it one of the "three sisters," a symbiotic planting of beans, squash, and corn. Their primitive pole beans climbed the tall cornstalks and helped their nitrogen-loving companions thrive by enriching the soil. Bean roots are hospitable to nitrogen-fixing bacteria, which absorb nitrogen gas from the atmosphere and convert it to a form that plants can use.

The reliable sisters continue to be a part of our gardens. From bush and pole snap beans to limas and dried beans, there are enough varieties to satisfy any gardener. Whether you prefer stringless, round-pod, or flat and broad Italian varieties; multicolored ones in yellows, purples, and greens; or dried beans of all stripes, beans command their place in the sunny garden. Some, such as the brilliantly flowered scarlet runner beans, have made the migration to the flower bed, where they bewitch hummingbirds and gardeners alike with their intensely red blossoms.

Today's gardeners have rediscovered many old-fashioned and heirloom varieties, such as the pole beans 'Jacob's Cattle' and 'Soldier', ideal for drying. Names like 'Kentucky Wonder' (a meaty-tasting pole snap bean) and 'Provider'

By replanting every two weeks throughout the growing season, you can greatly extend the length and scope of the annual bean harvest.

(a productive early-producing bush bean) conjure visions of harvests from homesteader gardens preserved in glass-topped canning jars to nourish families through long, cold winters.

No garden is too small to include beans. Even tiny balconies can host a productive mini-garden of the heirloom, heavy-yielding 'Bountiful Stringless' snap bean or a teepee of climbing, heirloom 'Garden of Eden' pole beans in a terra-cotta pot full of rich soil. Though beans do require warm, well-drained soil—at least 60°F, with a pH above 6.0—weather is hardly a concern for those people who desire to grow them. There are pole beans, such as 'Cascade Giant' stringless snap beans, that tolerate cool, damp weather and others, such as the skinny 'Yardlong', or 'Asparagus', beans that shrug off heat and drought to produce tender green beans that are as good in salads and cooked dishes as they are on their own. For a fiesta of color, try mixing 'Purple Queen', 'Goldkist', and 'Blue Lake' bush beans.

Edamame, fresh soybean pods, such as 'Envy', above, have long been a staple in Japan.

The broad, meaty fava bean (*Vicia faba*) provides a wealth of culinary possibilities, either used fresh or shelled out as a dried bean. This native of northern Europe prefers a cool growing environment. If summers are hot, try fava beans as an early-spring or fall crop.

Another bean that prefers mild weather is the nutritious edamame, as it is known in Japan. These green-seeded soy beans (*Glycine max*) ripen all at once on bushy, upright plants.

GROWING BEANS

Always select bean varieties that are suited to the climate and growing conditions in your area. Sow seeds directly in soil, following directions on the packet for planting depth and spacing. The large, easy-to-plant seeds and quick germination times (usually less than a week) make them a great first crop for young gardeners.

You can greatly extend the harvest by replanting every two weeks throughout the growing season. Harvest beans every day, while they are tender and small, for greatest flavor and to keep the plants in production.

Examine plants daily to ward off any pest or disease problems. Bean pests include the tiny (¼-inch long) orange Mexican bean beetle, recognizable by the 16 distinctive dark spots on its back. Try planting radishes alongside the beans, which will discourage beetles while enhancing the flavor of the beans. A patch of potato plants nearby may also help repel these pests. Or you can use the botanical insecticide pyrethrin to control the beetles. If aphids move in, plant nasturtiums between the rows, or place strips of aluminum foil flat on the ground under the plants. The foil is believed to "confuse" aphids, and it also reflects light up to the plants, giving them an added benefit.

Beans are also susceptible to a number of fungal diseases, including bean rust and bacterial bean blight, both of which respond well to spraying with a mixture of garlic juice and water (mix 1 part garlic juice to 20 parts water). Excessive watering can encourage the spread of fungus, especially when the foliage stays wet. A mulch of straw can help prevent foliage from coming in constant contact with moist soil. To protect future crops, remove all mulch or dead vegetation from the garden when the growing season is over, and rotate crops to help avoid diseases or pest infestations the following year. It is safe to compost most spent plants, but it's best to discard or burn those heavily infested with fungus or insects.

RECOMMENDED VARIETIES

Days to maturity listed below are counted from the time of planting seed.

'BUSH BLUE LAKE'—Bush; 58 days; tender green pods 6½ inches long; use fresh or for freezing.

'PURPLE QUEEN'—Bush; 55 days; vigorous, upright plants, 5½-inch tender, sweet, purple pods.

'ROMA'—Bush; 55 days; heavy producer of flat, tender 4½-inch green pods.

'ENVY'—Green soy bean (edamame); 75 days; short-season favorite on upright two-foot plants; good for eating fresh or shelled as dry beans.

'ASPARAGUS' ('YARDLONG')—Pole; 50 days; vigorous climbing vines; 18-inch slender and tender green pods with delicious nutty flavor; very heat-tolerant.

'CASCADE GIANT'—Pole; 65 days; heavy production of stringless, dark green pods mottled with purple; tolerates cool, damp weather.

'FORTEX'—Pole; 60 days; pick beans early for tender seven-inch green beans or allow to mature to 11 inches for firm-textured stringless beans.

'SPECKLED CRANBERRY'—Pole; 60 to 90 days; heirloom (England 1825); harvest heavy, early crops of seven- to nine-inch stringless pods for eating fresh; pick as fresh-shelled beans at 80 days and cook like fresh limas or grow to full maturity as dry beans, which are a distinctive nut-brown speckled with deep cranberry.

EATING BEANS

Beans are a good source of vitamins A and C, as well as calcium and iron. And they pair well with a number of herbs, especially basil and dill. For the best flavor and nutrition, pick beans right before you intend to cook them. Plunge them into a pot of boiling water and cook until they are just crisp-tender (about three minutes) to preserve their bright color and delicate flavor. Test the largest bean to see if it is tender. When they're done, quickly drain and toss the hot beans with a squirt of lemon juice, a dusting of fresh dill, and just enough olive oil to coat them. Don't be disappointed if your 'Purple Queen' beans turn green as they're cooking—that's what they do. But oh, what a lovely deep shade of green they are. And their perky flavor makes up for the loss of the unusual hue.

Nutritious, fresh edamame soy beans are easily cooked by steaming or boiling the whole pods for about five minutes. Cool the pods with a flush of cold water so the beans can be popped out of their fuzzy shells and eaten immediately. Edamame can also be packed for freezing at this point or returned to the pot for five to ten minutes of steaming before serving.

The large, late-season pole beans are best slow-cooked or simmered over low heat to bring out their hearty flavor. Large beans are a good choice for soups and stews. For shelled dried beans, pick fully mature beans before they are completely dry and spread on screens or layers of paper in the sun to prevent pods from getting mildewed. Most beans are well suited for freezing and canning, even pickling as dilly beans, but fresh from the garden is when beans shine their brightest.

GREEN BEANS WITH TOMATOES AND BASIL

1 pound small, tender green beans
2 tbsp. olive oil
2 cloves garlic, minced
1/4 cup fresh basil, chopped
2 medium fresh tomatoes, chopped
Freshly ground black pepper to taste

Clean and snap the stem ends off the beans and break the beans into bite-size pieces. Bring a large pot of water to a boil and add the beans. Boil briskly for three minutes and check the largest bean to see if it is crisp-tender. Cook them longer if necessary, but the beans should still be bright green. Drain them in a colander and set aside.

In a pot, sauté the garlic in olive oil until soft, about two minutes. Over high heat, add the basil and tomatoes, stirring as the tomatoes soften and create a light sauce; cook for about two minutes. Add the beans and toss to mix and reheat. Add black pepper if desired. Serves four. This is one of the best ways to get those finicky young eaters to try fresh green beans.

BEETS
Beta vulgaris
ROSALIND CREASY

Beets are earthy, sweet, vitamin-packed vegetables, and I adore them. Fortunately, my family loves them too, as I serve them often. Chard, spinach beets, and beets were all selected from the wild beet (*Beta vulgaris* ssp. *maritima*). The ancient Greeks and Romans grew both red and white beets; later, yellow beets became popular throughout Europe. In America, the colonists relied on the large, red "keeper" beets for food in early spring when the larder was getting low. Beets such as 'Winter Keeper' grow to eight inches across, yet remain tender and sweet. Traditionally, they were placed among the coals in the hearth and roasted. Though many traditional seed companies offer only red beets, specialty seed houses carry white and golden beets; some carry an Italian striped cultivar called 'Barbietola di Chioggia' ('Chioggia').

Beets grow to their succulent best under cool conditions. In most climates, they are planted in the spring for an early-summer crop. But in cool-summer areas where temperatures rarely climb above 85°F, they can be grown over the summer; in USDA Zones 8 and 9 they can also be sown in the fall and harvested in early spring.

GROWING BEETS

Generally, beets grow best in full sun, except in regions where temperatures regularly rise above 85°F by late spring or early summer. In that case, plant beets in a spot in the garden that gets afternoon shade.

Sow beet seeds in rich, fast-draining soil. You can mix the different-colored varieties in the same bed, but be aware that golden beets have poor germination rates, so sow more of them to compensate. Plant seeds ¼-inch deep in rows, or broadcast the seeds over a three-foot-wide bed. Thinning is critical to prevent stunted roots: Thin the seedlings of most varieties to three inches apart; thin large

Beets, such as the unusually shaped 'Cylindra', grow to their succulent best under cool conditions.

ROASTED BEET SALAD
WITH FALL GREENS AND FETA CHEESE

4 medium beets

Remove the tops of the beets and set aside. Wash roots and put them in a small casserole with a lid, no need to add water. Put the covered dish in the oven and bake at 300°F for about $1^1/_2$ hours or until tender. Remove beets from the oven, peel, and thinly slice or cut into strips. Refrigerate until ready to use.

VINAIGRETTE
1 tbsp. red wine vinegar
$^1/_2$ tsp. honey
4 tbsp. olive oil
2 tbsp. finely chopped fresh dill or fennel
Salt and freshly ground black pepper to taste

In a small bowl whisk together the vinegar, honey, and oil until well blended. Add the herbs and seasonings and set aside.

ASSEMBLING THE SALAD
4 handfuls of salad greens such as spinach, lettuce, and endive
$^1/_4$ pound feta cheese, crumbled
4 roasted beets, sliced or cut into strips
Vinaigrette

Put the greens in a large bowl and toss with three-quarters of the vinaigrette until they are evenly coated. Arrange the greens on a large serving plate. Put the beets in a small bowl, pour the rest of the dressing over them, and stir to coat. Arrange the beets over the greens. Sprinkle feta cheese over the salad and serve. Serves four to six.

storage beets to six inches apart. Once the beets are a few inches tall, apply an inch of organic mulch, such as compost or straw, to keep the roots cool. Fertilize the bed in midseason with a balanced organic fertilizer, and be sure to water regularly and deeply so that the roots grow evenly.

Occasionally, leafminers tunnel through beet leaves; you can control them by growing your crop under floating row covers. Two fungi cause orange spots on the foliage: *Cercospora* and a rust fungus. Grow beets in full sun and rotate beet crops to help cut down on pest infestations and diseases. Harvest most varieties when the roots are three inches in diameter or less.

Opposite: 'Barbietola di Chioggia' ('Chioggia'), an Italian beet variety, looks beautiful and tastes delicious, especially when roasted, as in the salad recipe on this page.

RECOMMENDED VARIETIES

Days to maturity listed below are counted from the time of planting seed.

'ACTION'—50 days; hybrid; bolt-resistant, sweet and tender.

'ALBINA VERDUNA'—65 days; Dutch heirloom; pure white, large, and sweet; has been used to make beet sugar.

'BURPEE'S GOLDEN'—60 days; sweet golden root that doesn't "bleed" and discolor other foods. Low germination rate, so plant extra seeds.

'BARBIETOLA DI CHIOGGIA' ('CHIOGGIA')—50 days; Italian heirloom; red on outside, white inside with red rings like a bull's eye; sweet.

'CYLINDRA' ('FORMANOVA')—60 days; dark red, long, cylindrical beet; good for slicing.

'DETROIT DARK RED'—60 days; heirloom; many strains available, some susceptible to *Cercospora* leaf spot; uniform in color and shape.

'LUTZ GREEN LEAF' ('WINTER KEEPER', 'LONG KEEPER')—80 days; heirloom; large reddish-purple root that is sweet and tender even when six inches across; for fall harvest and storage.

'RUBY QUEEN'—60 days; uniform shape; for home use and processing; AAS winner.

EATING BEETS

My favorite way to cook beets is roasting, sometimes with carrots and parsnips. I dress the roasted beets with butter and fresh herbs such as mint, dill, or fennel; I also add them to salads or marinate them in a vinaigrette as an appetizer. I think a bowl of steaming borscht makes a perfect supper on a cold evening, and when I have a large harvest, I often make pickled beets.

The rich flavor of beets is enhanced when they are combined with oranges, onions, walnuts, ginger, and mustard. I find beet greens a special treat steamed and served with butter or olive oil and garlic. For me, beets are real soul food.

Golden beets have poor germination rates, so sow more of them to compensate—they're definitely worth the extra effort.

CABBAGES AND OTHER BRASSICAS

ANNE RAVER

The world of brassicas is a lot bigger than cabbages for coleslaw. It includes the elegant savoys, whose puckered green leaves can stand up to cold weather, and 'January King', an old English cold-hardy giant cabbage with swirling blue leaves that could steal the heart of gardeners who think they loathe the stuff. And it includes a number of other crops that have been developed from the same species of wild cabbage native to the Mediterranean region, *Brassica oleracea:* delicious kales and collards, which can be picked as tender leaves for a mesclunlike salad or harvested when they are much larger and tougher, to be sautéed with plenty of garlic and a pinch of hot pepper or simmered slowly, southern-style, with some salty ham.

Black kale, which has long, narrow dark green curled and wrinkled leaves, has been used in Tuscany for centuries to make a satisfying winter soup. It is variously called Tuscan kale, palm cabbage, or even dinosaur kale. English gardener Joy Larkcom notes in *Creative Vegetable Gardening* (Abbeville, 1997) that Vilmorin-Andrieux, the French seed company that flourished in the 18th and 19th centuries and produced the popular 1885 book *The Vegetable Garden,* praised black kale's elegant appearance in the garden. This perennial can grow for three years in mild areas, finally flowering at about five feet. Larkcom, a master of ornamental vegetable gardening, grows black kale as an annual, in the center or at the corners of a bed, or interplants it with radicchio and red lettuce. Then there are brussels sprouts, which get sweeter in the snow, and cauliflowers and broccolis, including that oddball, lime-

Pak choi is a tasty Asian contribution to the many-branched family of brassicas.

Elegant savoy cabbage can stand up to cold weather. In the fall, decorative cabbage varieties have moved successfully from the vegetable patch to the flower garden.

green, spiraling Romanesco type, which looks like the offspring of both.

Another species, *Brassica rapa*, is the origin of broccoli raab, with multiple stems, spicy leaves, and flower buds combining the flavors of mustard greens and broccoli, Chinese cabbage, and Asian greens like pak choi, mizuna, and tatsoi. The species *Brassica juncea* has given us all those mustards that add spicy, hot flavors to an early spring salad, along with colors ranging from grass-green to purple (see "Salad Greens," page 84).

GROWING CABBAGE

Cabbages need fertile, well-limed soil, with a pH above 6, and plenty of moisture. Sow early and mid-season varieties indoors, six weeks before the last frost. Seeds germinate best at 75°F, but seedlings grown under lights thrive in a cool room kept at about 60°F. Plant outdoors, one foot apart. Fall crops should be started in May and transplanted from June to July.

Brussels sprouts may be started in pots in May or sown directly in outdoor beds, seeds spaced three to four inches apart, in rows 30 inches apart. Transplant or thin to 18 inches apart in four to six weeks. Sprouts mature in 100 to 125 days. When the sprouts form, pinch the tips of the plants to promote fat sprouts. After the first hard frost, the sprouts get sweeter, but if temperatures fall below 20°F, pull the plants and store them in a root cellar. The sprouts will be good for several weeks; if the roots are planted in damp sand and it doesn't get too cold, the sprouts can last a few months.

Black kale, 'Lacinato', above, has been used in Tuscan cooking for centuries. Nutritious, versatile, and relatively cold-hardy, kale is a staple in many regional cuisines.

Broccoli raab is fast-growing and vigorous; it can be used as a cut-and-come-again green or harvested when the plants are mature. This green needs fertile soil and lots of moisture. Adapted to short days, it tends to bolt when sown in spring or early summer, so plant the seeds directly in the garden in midsummer to early fall. Protect plants from flea beetles and caterpillars with row covers. If you must have raab in the spring (as I do), choose a bolt-resistant variety and plant as early as possible.

Chinese cabbage is easy to grow if you choose bolt-resistant varieties for spring crops and don't plant out before night temperatures rise above 50°F. Cover seedlings with floating row covers to prevent flea beetles and root maggots. Midsummer and fall crops may be direct sown in late May through late July.

RECOMMENDED VARIETIES

BRASSICA OLERACEA

HEAD CABBAGE

Days to maturity listed below are counted from the time of transplanting.

'CHIEFTAIN SAVOY'—83 days; introduced in 1938; tolerates frost as well as summer heat; blistered blue-green leaves surround the white head, which can weigh six to eight pounds.

'EARLY JERSEY WAKEFIELD'—65 days; heirloom; one of the best-tasting cabbages around; small, pointed heads.

Like all brassicas, broccoli needs fertile soil and plenty of moisture. Above is the rather striking Romanesco type, with its whorls of lime-green florets.

'KILOSA'—72 days; savoy type; tender crinkled leaves; good taste that improves with cold weather.

'PRIMAX' OR 'GOLDEN ACRE'—60 days; early, small, light green head with dark green leaves; a favorite for coleslaw and stir-frying.

'REGAL RED'—78 days; beautiful mid-season cabbage; good taste.

'ROULETTE'—105 days; fall and winter type; medium-size, blue-green head; thin, tasty leaves; tolerates freezing weather.

BRUSSELS SPROUTS
Days to maturity listed below are counted from the time of transplanting.

'CATSKILL' OR 'LONG ISLAND IMPROVED'—90 days; introduced in 1941; compact plant 20 inches tall; sustained production; widely adapted.

'HARLEY'—110 days; Dutch hybrid; tall plants with great-tasting buds; resistant to *Fusarium* wilt.

'JADE CROSS'—80 days; blue-green sprouts; adapted to wide range of soils; early and productive.

'OLIVER'—90 days; vigorous; easy to grow; early sprouts; can sow seed in mid-summer and still get a crop.

KOHLRABI
Days to maturity listed below are counted from the time of planting seed.

'EDER'—38 days; extra early; white; very tender.

'KOLIBRI'—45 days; large bulbs; deep purple skin, white flesh.

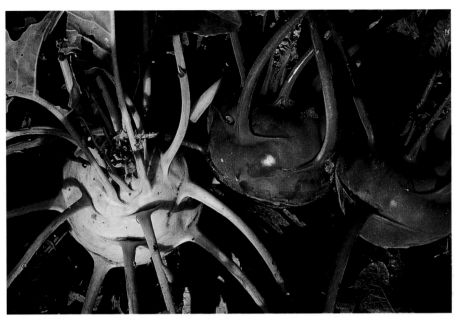

Along with head cabbages, Brussels sprouts, broccoli, cauliflower, collards, and kale, kohlrabi, above, has been developed from *Brassica oleracea,* a wild Mediterranean cabbage.

'LOGO'—45 days; white; European favorite for baby vegetables.

'WINNER'—45 days; white; sweet taste.

'WHITE VIENNA'—50 days; heirloom; sweet and crunchy.

BROCCOLI
Days to maturity listed below are counted from the time of transplanting.

'CALABRESE' OR 'ITALIAN GREEN SPROUTING'—58 days; heavy producer; large green heads; cut the main head, then enjoy side sprouts for weeks.

'DE CICCO'—49 days; introduced in 1890; three- to six-inch heads with side sprouts; use young leaves like collard greens once head is partly developed.

'GREEN COMET'—40 days; AAS Gold Medal winner; early maturing; good for beginners; large, six- to seven-inch heads.

ROMANESCO—about 80 days; Romanesco type; lime-green spiraled heads; best planted in summer for fall crop; nutty flavor; gorgeous oddball.

'PREMIUM CROP'—62 days; AAS Gold Medal winner; large, six- to nine-inch compact heads; resistant to heat and *Fusarium* wilt; good fall crop.

CAULIFLOWER
Days to maturity listed below are counted from the time of transplanting.

'SNOW CROWN'—50 days; early; easy to grow.

'FREMONT'—62 days; easy to grow; adaptable to wide variety of soils; big leaves make it a self-blancher.

'VIOLET QUEEN'—54 days; easy to grow; purple florets; intermediate between

PORTUGUESE KALE SOUP

1 cup dried red beans
$^1/_4$ pound salt pork
$^1/_2$ pound beef shank (or 2 ham hocks)
5 cloves garlic, minced
1 large onion, chopped
3 quarts water
3 large potatoes, cut into small pieces
4 to 6 cups chopped kale (bitter stems removed)
$^1/_2$ pound linguiça sausage
1 bunch scallions, chopped (optional)
1 chile pepper, chopped (optional garnish)
Freshly grated Parmesan
Salt and pepper to taste

Rinse beans, then soak overnight. In the morning, rinse and drain. Sauté salt pork, minced garlic, and chopped onion in bottom of a stockpot. Add three quarts water, beef shanks or ham hocks, and dried beans. Simmer for three hours or until beans are edible but not yet soft. Add potatoes and kale; simmer until tender. Brown linguiça, slice thinly, and add to soup. Cook for ten minutes more. Put chopped scallions, chopped chile pepper, and freshly grated Parmesan in little serving bowls for those who like an even zestier flavor. Serves six.

cauliflower and broccoli; turns light green when blanched.

COLLARDS

Days to maturity listed below are counted from the time of planting seed.

'CHAMPION'—75 days; rich dark green leaves; slow-bolting, very productive.

'GREEN GLAZE'—79 days; heirloom; bright green smooth leaves; heat and frost-resistant; resistant to cabbage worm.

'VATES'—68 days; large blue-green leaves; 32-inch-tall plant; frost-resistant.

KALE

Days to maturity listed below are counted from the time of planting seed.

'LACINATO'—30 days for tender greens, 65 mature; Tuscan black cabbage; two-foot-long strap-shaped leaves; tolerant of hot or cold weather; mild flavor that's great for soup.

'VATES DWARF BLUE'—55 days; curly kale; can overwinter in mid-Atlantic region; very flavorful.

'RED RUSSIAN'—40 days for baby leaves, 50 days mature; mild flavor; blue-green toothed leaves that turn purplish-red with the cold; can grow to two feet.

'RAGGED JACK'—48 days; similar to Red Russian but grows to 14 inches.

'REDBOR'—45 days; deep purple curly leaves; large plants; sweetens with frost.

WILD KALE MIX—Mix of diverse shapes and colors; great for cut-and-come-again salads; sow seeds in late spring and let them grow to full height or sow through the summer and use for cut-and-come-again salads.

BRASSICA RAPA

BROCCOLI RAAB

Days to maturity listed below are counted from the time of planting seed.

'SESSATINA GROSSA'—35 days; large early buds; spring, fall, and winter crop.

'SPRING RAAB'—42 days, slow to bolt; good for spring and summer harvest; over-winter for spring crop.

CHINESE CABBAGE
Days to maturity listed below are counted from the time of planting seed.

NAPA TYPES:

'MINUET'—48 days; small heads with dark green outer leaves, yellow interior; light sweet taste.

'BLUES'—50 days; bolt-resistant; tall heads with white interior; sweet, juicy.

MICHIHILI TYPE:

Collards are very cold-resistant. Above is 'Vates'.

'GREENWICH'—50 days; elegant 14-inch-tall, firm, narrow heads; dark green curled and wrinkled outer leaves.

KOMATSUNA GROUP:

'KOMATSUNA SUMMER FEST'—35 days; heat-resistant greens; mild and tender, delicious for salads and stir-frying.

PURPLE-FLOWERED CHOY SUM:

'HON TSAI TAI'—37 days; tender pencil-thin purplish-red stems and yellow buds; mustardy taste.

PAK CHOI, BOK CHOI:

'AUTUMN POEM'—35 days; flowering pak choi type; glossy deep green leaves; tender buds; stems taste like broccoli.

'CHINESE PAK CHOI'—50 days; thick glossy leaves; crisp stems; 16- to 20-inch plants.

'MEI QUING PAK CHOI'—45 days; flat greenish-white stems; snugly packed; rich green oval leaves.

'JOI CHOI'—50 days; 12- to 25-inch-tall plants; thick white stems with dark green leaves.

TATSOI—45 days; deep green spoon-shaped leaves that form a rosette; late-spring through autumn sowing; mild taste.

EATING CABBAGES

I like to stir-fry most of the leafy brassicas in good olive oil, chopped garlic, and a bit of hot pepper. Don't add salt until the stems are al dente and ready to serve; if you add it earlier, your greens will be soggy. Pak choi is delicious sautéed in peanut oil; Chinese mustard greens are good with fresh ginger rather than garlic.

CARROTS
Daucus carota
ELIZABETH BURGER

What is it about carrots that so fascinates me? Maybe it has to do with pulling up a little orange surprise, a succulent, sweet treasure that was hidden in the earth. Once you have tasted a carrot that was grown organically, you will be reluctant to make do with the supermarket variety. One crop harvested from your own vegetable garden, and you will know why it's best to grow them yourself.

Along with parsnips, celery, fennel, and parsley, the carrot belongs to the Apiaceae, or carrot family, which until recently was known as the Umbelliferae. Carrots are biennial, producing a delicious taproot in their first year and flowers and seeds in their second year.

Probably originating from the environs of modern-day Afghanistan, the roots, distantly related to Queen Anne's lace (*Anthriscus sylvestris*), have been with us for millennia. Seeds have been found at neolithic sites in Switzerland, and carrots are mentioned in Sanskrit texts from India and in the sixth-century Codex of Dioscorides from Constantinople. The Romans grew them. Apicius, the first-century Roman cookery writer, gives a recipe for *carota sue pastinaca*, which uses more or less the carrot we know today.

Carrots are rich in beta-carotene, the naturally occurring form of vitamin A thought to help prevent cancer. Apart from beets, carrots have more natural sugar than any other vegetable. According to William Woys Weaver's book *100 Vegetables and Where They Came From*, carrot seeds possess a number of medicinal uses that are well documented in old herbals, such as cleansing the kidneys, easing difficult breathing, and discharging phlegm from the chest. Carrots also may lower the risk of heart disease and stroke, and yes, they help prevent glaucoma. Your mother was right: Eat carrots.

And with names like 'Chantenay', 'Touchon', 'Bolero', 'Kinko', 'White Belgium', 'Scarlet Nantes', 'Thumbelina', 'Oxheart', 'Parmex', 'Rondo', and 'St. Valery', who can resist? All promise instant health and a chance to practice French in the garden (many of today's sweet, improved varieties were developed in France).

Humans aren't the only ones keenly interested in carrots, though. Rabbits will do anything to get at them. If you like skirmishes in the garden, this vegetable is a must. This year, I planned carefully, reinforcing the snow fence I use to encircle my garden with one-inch chicken wire. I thought I was invincible until some very smart bunny found a weak spot and tunneled in. Keeping up with bunny ingenuity does make the daily inspection tour more interesting. By reinforcing each little opening, you can stem the invasion.

Opposite: Growing cool-weather-loving carrots next to their favorite companions, onions and tomatoes, helps repel insect pests.

GROWING CARROTS

I grow my carrots next to their favorite companions, onions and tomatoes, because folklore and many garden books suggest these plants repel carrot-loving insects. Carrots will do well in heavy, clay soil as long as you work in sand, compost, and a little lime. Generally, the shorter varieties work better in heavy soil. If you prefer the longer types, soil preparation is a must.

Carrots love cool weather and can be started as soon as all danger of frost has passed. At planting time, mix radish seeds into the bed, as they will come up first and remind you where your carrots are. If root maggots attack, they will go for the radishes first. And save those coffee grounds, which are good for the roots. Sprinkle some around the plants every few weeks and water them in.

To aid germination, keep the carrot bed well watered. Thinning several times until the carrots are spaced four inches apart will provide you with a first flush of babies to put in salads and stews, but the carrots will be more nutritious as they mature and develop terpenes, which give them their flavor. If you can, mulch some carrots well in the fall and leave them in the ground over the winter; you can eat them through the spring, when they will be even sweeter. Putting carrots up for storage is not difficult either: Moist sand between layers of healthy plants (with the tops removed) will keep carrots crisp for up to six months. Ideally, the temperature for storage should hover around 32°F, with a relative humidity of 95 percent.

RECOMMENDED VARIETIES

Days to maturity listed below are counted from the time of planting seed.

'BOLERO'—75 days; thick and blunt; seven to eight inches long; great for late-fall crop and winter storage; big tops withstand blight.

'CHANTENAY'—70 days; deep orange, 6½ to 7½ inches long; incredibly sweet and crisp.

'PARMEX'—50 days; small round Parisian market carrot; early, harvest at 1½ inches for sweetest taste.

'KINKO'—52 days; an early Chantenay type; small and conical with deep red-orange color inside and out; best harvested young, at about two inches; good for heavy soil.

'SCARLET NANTES'—70 days; slim, cylindrical, six to eight inches long with rounded top; fine-grained, nearly coreless; makes a great baby gourmet vegetable.

CARROTS VICHY

½ pound carrots, thinly sliced
½ cup boiling water
2 tbsp. butter
1 tbsp. sugar
¼ tsp. salt
1 tsp. lemon juice (optional)
Parsley as garnish

Place all the ingredients in a saucepan and cover the pan closely. Simmer the carrots until the water is absorbed and a glaze has formed. Serve sprinkled with parsley. Serves four.

CAROTTES À LA CONCIERGE

$1^1/_2$ pounds carrots, cut into $^1/_4$-inch slices
$1^1/_2$ cups onions, sliced
4 tbsp. olive oil
1 large clove garlic, mashed
1 tbsp. flour
$^1/_4$ cup brown or vegetable stock, brought to a boil
$^3/_4$ cup boiling milk
1 tsp. sugar
Salt and pepper
Pinch of nutmeg
2 egg yolks
4 tbsp. whipping cream
2 tbsp. minced parsley

Cook the carrots, onions, and olive oil slowly in a covered $2^1/_2$-quart heavy-bottomed saucepan, tossing occasionally, for about 30 minutes. Vegetables should be tender but not browned. Add the garlic for the last five minutes of cooking. Toss the vegetables with the flour and cook for three more minutes.

Take the pan off the heat and slowly add the boiling stock, then the milk, and finally the sugar and seasonings. Simmer uncovered for about 20 minutes, or until the liquid has reduced to a third of its volume, thickening to a light cream. Meanwhile, in a bowl, blend the egg yolks and whipping cream.

Just before serving, remove the carrots from the heat and use a spatula to fold in the egg yolks and cream. Shake the pan over low heat until the egg yolks have thickened, but do not bring them near simmer or they may coagulate. Sprinkle with parsley and serve.

Serves six as a side dish with red meat, pork, sausages, or roast chicken. Serves four as a hearty main dish.

'TOUCHON'—75 days; originated in France; six to eight inches long; almost coreless; bright orange center; finest juice carrot.

EATING CARROTS

Although I prefer eating carrots raw, I also have found that combining them with potatoes, parsley, beets, peppers, beans, rutabagas, and other vegetables in soups maintains their flavor, and texture, provided they are not overcooked. To retain nutrients and strong flavor, prepare carrots in a vegetable steamer. If you want the most delicious sweet cake, to be eaten at any time of the day, make carrot cake, adding walnuts and raisins. And what would gazpacho be without carrots?

CHARD
Beta vulgaris var. cicla
RENEE SHEPHERD

One of my favorite garden staples, chard is ornamental, easy to grow, long-harvesting, nutritious, and incredibly versatile in the kitchen. I think this handsome leafy vegetable is undervalued by most of us. Native to the Mediterranean region, where it has been grown since classical antiquity, chard is closely related to beets, spinach, and spinach beets, fellow members of the goosefoot family, Chenopodiaceae. It is, in fact, also known as leaf beet, and more commonly in North America, as Swiss chard.

Many-leafed, vase-shaped chard plants grow upright to about two feet tall and produce large, broad, slightly crinkled leaves on crunchy, fleshy stalks. Both leaves and stalks are edible. The tender, bright green leaves are good raw in salads when very young, about three or four inches long, but need cooking as they mature. Chard has a flavor reminiscent of spinach, but it is earthier and has more body.

A cut-and-come-again vegetable, chard will continue to replace harvested leaves with new growth.

GROWING CHARD

Plant chard in spring and harvest in summer, or plant in midsummer for a fall crop. Sow seeds directly in well-worked fertile soil in full sun. Firm the soil well over the irregularly shaped seeds to ensure germination. If the first sowing germinates unevenly, plant more seed, as new seedlings will catch up quickly. Thin the seedlings carefully, spacing them 12 inches apart, as the plants grow large and need plenty of room. Once well established, chard can withstand both summer heat and light frost.

You can begin harvesting when the plants have six to eight stalks. Pick leaves from the outside of the plant, snapping the stalks at their bases. Chard is a cut-and-come-again vegetable that will continue to replace harvested leaves with new growth for weeks. Few plants yield more per square foot of garden space than this unfussy, tasty vegetable.

There are wonderful varieties that are as highly ornamental as they are good to eat. One of the most beautiful and widely available is actually a venerable variety, All-America Award–winning 'Bright Lights', recently reselected for color and flavor. Its stalks come in a vivid rainbow of yellow, crimson, gold, pink, and white, with an occasional gorgeous stem of orange, and its leaves are mild and sweet. Several Italian chards are also available from good seed sources. They have broad silver or pale green juicy stalks that contrast handsomely with big, tender green leaves, which are also mild and delicious. 'Rhubarb', or 'Ruby Red', chard is another old favorite with American gar-

'Rhubarb' ('Ruby Red') is one of the highly ornamental varieties of chard.

deners. This vivid beauty has deep magenta stalks, complemented by red-veined, deep green, deeply curled and wrinkled leaves.

RECOMMENDED VARIETIES

Days to maturity listed below are counted from the time of planting seed.

'ITALIAN SILVER RIB'—60 days; handsome, vigorous plants with wide silvery midribs and crinkly broad deep green leaves; selected by discerning Italian cooks for its clean, mellow flavor; great spinach alternative.

'BRIGHT LIGHTS'—60 days; highly ornamental; tender, mild- and sweet-tasting stalks in a rainbow of colors; succulent dark green leaves.

'RHUBARB' ('RUBY RED')—60 days; deep crimson stalks, crinkled green leaves.

'SILVERADO'—55 days; dark green, deeply curled and wrinkled leaves.

'LARGE WHITE RIBS'—60 days; white stems with thick leaves that are tender and delicious; cook the entire stem and leaf or steam stems like asparagus.

'LUCULLUS'—50 days; introduced in 1914; named after the Roman general

Lucius Lucullus, renowned for his lavish banquets; pale green leaves with heavily crumpled leaves.

'RAINBOW'—60 days; originally from Australia; multicolored plants in shades of red, orange, pink, yellow, and cream.

'FORDHOOK GIANT'—60 days; broad dark green leaves, thick white stems.

EATING CHARD

If you've only eaten bitter, metallic-tasting supermarket chard, you are in for a pleasant surprise; homegrown varieties are much more sweet and flavorful. When preparing chard, I usually separate the stalks from the leaves, because the stalks have a different texture than the leaves and cook more slowly. The leaves can be steamed, stir-fried, braised, or baked, used in soups and pasta dishes, or substituted for spinach in lasagna. They are the perfect size to blanch and use as wrappers for your favorite fillings, or they can be poached in broth with a dash of olive oil. Best of all, chard is wonderful as an everyday side dish, simply braised in a little olive oil and sprinkled with fresh lemon juice or topped with grated Parmesan.

MILANESE-STYLE CHARD

1 pound Swiss chard
2 tbsp. olive oil
1 clove garlic, minced
6 scallions, thinly sliced
2 tbsp. fresh parsley, chopped
1/4 cup fresh basil, chopped
pinch nutmeg
1/4 cup prosciutto or ham, chopped
2 tbsp. Parmesan cheese, grated
Salt and freshly ground pepper to taste
2 tbsp. pine nuts or chopped walnuts, toasted

Trim the chard, discarding tough stems, and coarsely chop. In a large, deep skillet, heat the olive oil; add the garlic and scallions and sauté until softened and fragrant, two to three minutes. Add the chard, parsley, basil, nutmeg, and prosciutto or ham and mix together well. Cover the skillet and cook over medium heat until the chard is tender and wilted, three to five minutes. Mix in the Parmesan cheese and add salt and pepper to taste. Serve garnished with the pine nuts or walnuts. Serves four to six.

This recipe is adapted from *Recipes From a Kitchen Garden,* by Renee Shepherd and Fran Raboff (Ten Speed Press, 1993).

CORN
Zea mays
ANNE RAVER

Domesticated in Mexico, corn has been in cultivation for at least 5,500 years. It was a sacred crop to the Native Americans, who treasured the distinctive patterns of the various types, carefully selecting the finest corns and passing them on to the next generation.

Thanks to these careful seed savers—who not only gave corn to the colonists but also taught them how to plant it—we still have a great variety of corns, from popcorn, the earliest and hardiest, to starchy dent corn, which is best roasted or made into hominy or corn bread, to the softer types that are eaten green, in the milky stage, or ground into flour when the kernels are hard and mature.

Sweet corn comes in many forms, from old-time hybrids like 'Silver Queen' to the new super-sweet varieties that don't start turning to starch as soon as you pick them. But to me, the new ones taste like white sugar. They have lost that satisfying corn flavor. I think of them as junk food.

I grew up in a family that loved to grow corn, and my mother really did put the proverbial pot on the stove and tell us to run down to the field and pick a peck of 'Silver Queen' or 'Golden Bantam'. I know the feel of those thick scratchy leaves against my face as I reached up and ripped off the ears and then ran back to the house with my sister, the pan clanking between us. We would yank off the husks on the porch, gouging out the occasional worm with a penknife, and hand the ears on a platter through the door to my mother. She

'Silver Queen', an old-time corn hybrid, is best eaten as soon as it is picked.

would toss a tablespoon of salt into the boiling water, drop in the ears, and three minutes later we'd be smothering them with butter, salt, and pepper. Like lost youth, I don't think I'll ever regain that flavor, intensified by memory, but I have grown many different corns since then. And I still put the pot on to boil before I go out to the corn patch.

GROWING CORN

Corn is wind-pollinated, and since all corn varieties belong to the same species, they easily cross-pollinate when the wind blows across the tassels of one variety, carrying pollen to the silks of another. So if you want more than one type of corn, you will have to plant one variety 100 feet upwind from another, or stagger the plantings by about two weeks so that the tassels shed their pollen at different times.

Corn is a nitrogen guzzler, so work plenty of compost and aged manure into well-draining soil. Wait until the soil temperature reaches at least 65°F before planting, as the seeds won't germinate in cool soil. Plant corn in blocks of at least five rows for proper pollination, sowing two to three seeds one inch deep, eight to ten inches apart in rows about 30 inches apart. Thin to one seedling.

I have also planted heirloom varieties the way the native Americans first taught the settlers: with a fish head in each hole and pole beans planted around each stalk. Wait until the corn is about eight inches high before planting the beans, which will wind up the stalk. Then plant squash or pumpkins between the rows. The nitrogen from the beans is supposed to help feed the corn, and the scratchy squash vines

SHAKER GREEN CORN PUDDING

2 cups grated green corn
3 eggs
$^1/_4$ cup sugar
dash of grated nutmeg
$^1/_2$ tsp. salt
$^1/_8$ tsp. ground pepper
2 cups milk
$^1/_2$ cup soft fresh bread crumbs swirled in melted butter
2 tbsp. butter

Preheat the oven to 250°F. Place the corn in a buttered baking dish. Beat the eggs and add the sugar, nutmeg, salt, pepper, and milk; blend. Pour the mixture over the corn and sprinkle with buttered bread crumbs. Dot with butter. Set the baking dish in a pan of boiling water and bake for one hour. Serves six.

My grandmother, Edith Moore, used to make corn pudding, but I never got her recipe. This one, from Craig Claiborne, is about as close as I could get. I use less sugar, about a teaspoon. If you like it hot, add a minced chile pepper. Green corn means fresh corn, in the milky stage.

are supposed to discourage raccoons. I don't know if it worked or if I just got lucky that year, but no raccoons ravaged my corn. The lovely blossoms of the scarlet runner beans festooned the stalks, and the beans produced until frost.

Keep corn earworms in check by putting up bat houses and bird boxes to attract predators; corn borers can be discouraged by clearing the beds of old cornstalks in fall and by rotating the crops, especially with beans, which put nitrogen back into the soil. I don't mind a worm or two, but Southern Exposure Seed Exchange, one of my favorite mail-order companies, recommends this deterrent: Insert a dropper half-filled with mineral oil into the silk of each ear after it has wilted and browned at the tip. Worms can also be killed with *Bt,* or *Bacillus thuringiensis,* but this kills butterflies too.

To frustrate raccoons, Mike Conover, a Connecticut agricultural extension agent, uses good old wrapping tape. Just after the pollen has fertilized the ears and kernels begin to develop, circle each ear once with ¾-inch fiberglass tape, about one inch above the area where it attaches to the stalk, then wind the tape once around the stalk, finishing with a circle of tape 1½ inches below the tip of the ear. I've never tried it, but Southern Exposure claims a 94 percent success rate.

RECOMMENDED VARIETIES

Days to maturity listed below are counted from the time of planting seed.

'BABY CORN'—18 days; sweet, creamy three-inch ears; perfect for sautéing or tossing into salads.

'GOLDEN BANTAM'—78 days; open-pollinated yellow corn introduced in 1902 by Burpee; 6½-inch ears on six-foot stalks; short milk stage, so pick immediately; real corn taste.

'OAXACAN GREEN'—90 to 100 days; heirloom dent corn that harks back to the Zapotec Indians of Oaxaca, Mexico; ears six to eight inches long on six-foot stalks; kernels vary from chartreuse to green-blue and can be ground at maturity into green flour for tamales.

'SILVER QUEEN'—92 days; old-time hybrid with sweet white kernels; 8½-inch ears on 7½-foot stalks; drought-tolerant and insect-resistant; this one insists on warm soil, so don't rush.

'STRAWBERRY POPCORN'—105 days; two-inch ears on four-foot stalks; mahogany-red kernels; highly resistant to corn earworm.

'TEXAS HONEY JUNE'—97 days; heirloom 6½-inch ears on eight-foot stalks; true corn flavor; tight husks discourage earworms.

EATING CORN

Get the pot boiling, toss in some salt, and cook the ears three minutes. Smother the corn with butter, salt, and pepper and eat it typewriter style or in a circular fashion. Slathering the ears with pesto is also acceptable. If you have any corn left over (it's doubtful), cut the kernels off the cobs and mix with fresh lima beans for succotash.

EGGPLANTS
Solanum melongena
JOAN JACKSON

Names can be misleading, and such is the case with the eggplant, so called because its fruit was originally small, whitish, and egg-shaped. Well, things sure have changed. Today's eggplants may be elongated or round. Their colors bear more resemblance to dyed Easter eggs than the straight-from-the-chicken kind. The most familiar eggplants are a deep purple-black color. But they also come in pink, cream, violet, or combinations of these hues. Cultivated for centuries, eggplants probably originated in India and were carried to Spain by Arab traders in the Middle Ages. By the 18th century, they had spread all over Europe. And like their relative the tomato, eggplants were considered ornamental curiosities well into the 19th century. Now, eggplants are still a beautiful addition to the summer garden. Mediterranean varieties are usually shaped like teardrops, ovals, or fat cylinders and are most often purple. Asian eggplants, also known as Japanese eggplants, are slender, elongated, and cylindrical, growing on compact bushes that produce relatively small fruits.

GROWING EGGPLANTS

Like tomatoes, eggplants are tender perennials grown as annuals. They need a long, hot growing season—three to four months of warm weather—to produce well and are especially sensitive to low temperatures. Start eggplants from seed indoors in March, sowing seeds ¼-inch deep and keeping the soil moist and warm (80°F to 85°F). The seeds will germinate in 10 to 15 days. Transplant out-doors eight weeks later, in May, when the soil temperature is at least 60°F and the air temperature is consistently above 70°F. In the garden, set the seedlings 18 to 24 inches apart. They don't like weeds, and they don't like to be crowded by other plants. Eggplants prefer a very rich soil, even watering, and regular doses of organic fertilizer, such as compost tea or fish emulsion applied every week until the first blooms appear. They thrive in hot weather and are even some-what drought-tolerant. Provide a generous mulch to keep their roots cool. They are prone to flea beetles and other small-insect attacks, but they will often grow through them, provided they have sufficient nourishment and water. Protect plants with floating row covers if pests get out of hand. Stake the big, vigorous eggplants, as the branches are brittle and may break under a heavy load of fruit. Wire tomato cages work well for this purpose. Not enough heat for a long grow-ing season? Pick Asian varieties that are labeled for short seasons and/or cover the bed with black plastic and plant the seedlings through holes cut into the plas-tic. Eggplants have the undeserved reputation of tasting bitter or seedy, but this happens only when the fruit becomes overly ripe. Harvest them when the skin is taut and shiny, and the fruit is firm to the touch.

Opposite: Until the 19th century, eggplants were considered ornamental curiosities.

SWEET AND SOUR EGGPLANT

2 medium eggplants, sliced $1/2$-inch thick, then quartered
Salt
2 tbsp. olive or other vegetable oil
1 large clove garlic, finely chopped
2 tbsp. sugar
2 tbsp. red wine vinegar

Salt the eggplant pieces and let them drain for 30 minutes; then rinse and pat dry. Heat the oil in a large, heavy skillet and add the garlic and eggplant. Sauté, stirring, until tender, about eight to ten minutes. Sprinkle the eggplant with sugar, turn, and continue to cook briefly until the sugar begins to caramelize. Add the vinegar and stir to blend. Serve immediately. Serves four. An easily prepared dish that really highlights the flavor of fresh-picked eggplants.

RECOMMENDED VARIETIES

Days to maturity listed below are counted from the time of planting seed.

'BLACK BEAUTY'—70 to 75 days; popular Mediterranean; oblong, eight- to ten-inch fruit; black with cream-white flesh.

'GREEN TIGER'—70 to 75 days; Thai; one- to two-inch round fruit; pale green striped with darker green.

'ITALIAN WHITE'—70 to 75 days; Mediterranean; round, plump, white to very pale green fruit; ripens earlier in the season; creamier and less bitter than purple types.

'LITTLE FINGERS'—60 days; hybrid from California; clusters of purple fruit shaped like long, fat fingers; early-bearing, vigorous producer.

'NEON'—70 days; Asian hybrid; dark pink, almost cylindrical fruit; bears very early, great for short-season gardens; not as bitter as some eggplants.

'OSTEREI'—70 to 75 days; German hybrid; small, oval white fruit; well suited for container gardens.

'PINGTUNG'—70 to 75 days; Taiwanese; slender lavender to purple fruit, up to one foot long.

'ROSA BIANCA'—75 days; Mediterranean; plump, teardrop-shaped fruit in shades of rosy lavender and soft white; creamy, mild without any bitterness.

'SLIM JIM'—75 days; unique to U.S. market; clusters of small lavender fruit; good for container culture; very ornamental.

EATING EGGPLANTS

For traditional Mediterranean dishes like eggplant parmigiana, the big, plump teardrop-shaped eggplants are best because they make nice fat slices. For stir-frying and grilling, the Asian eggplants are ideal, because they have thin skins, succulent flesh, and can easily be cut into even pieces. 'Green Tiger', for example, is good for stuffing, pickling, or stir-frying.

FENNEL
Foeniculum vulgare var. dulce
RENEE SHEPHERD

This delicately flavored vegetable, also known as finocchio or Florence fennel, is a traditional Italian culinary mainstay. Recipes for fennel go all the way back to Roman times, and the vegetable is also a part of ancient Greek and French cooking traditions.

A striking, pale green, two-foot-tall plant that forms a solid bulblike base the size of a tennis ball right at soil level, fennel has overlapping celerylike stems topped by feathery green fronds. It's important to distinguish this fleshy vegetable from the herb fennel (*Foeniculum vulgare* var. *vulgare*): the anise-flavored leaves and seeds of that non-bulbing herb are used as a flavoring throughout the temperate world.

GROWING FENNEL

Fennel needs rich soil, full sun, and cool weather to grow tender, top-quality bulbs. In cold-winter areas, start the seeds indoors six to eight weeks before the last frost date, using a sterile mix. Keep the mix moist and provide the seedlings with at least 12 hours of artificial light per day until they are well established and ready for transplanting; they should be two to three inches tall, with a set or two of true leaves. As soon as the soil can be worked and all danger of frost is over,

FENNEL AND PEA SAUTÉ

4 or 5 medium fennel bulbs
2 tbsp. olive oil
1 medium onion, chopped
2 tbsp. lemon juice
1 tsp. fresh tarragon, chopped
1$^1/_2$ cups peas (If using frozen peas, defrost partially before using.)
Salt and freshly ground pepper to taste

Cut off the fennel tops, reserving the feathery leaves for garnish. Slice the bulbs into thin strips. In a large skillet heat the oil and add the onion and fennel. Sauté, stirring occasionally, for five minutes, until tender-crisp. Add the lemon juice, tarragon, and peas, and cook five minutes more until the peas and fennel are just tender. Add salt and pepper to taste. Sprinkle with the chopped fennel tops just before serving. Serves six.

This recipe is adapted from *More Recipes From a Kitchen Garden*, by Renee Shepherd and Fran Raboff (Ten Speed Press, 1995).

transplant the seedlings to the garden bed, spacing them 10 to 12 inches apart. (You can sow the seeds directly outdoors, but it's more difficult, as the seedlings are small and the feathery leaves can be hard to see. Don't forget to thin them for proper spacing.) In areas where winter temperatures don't go much below 26°F or 27°F, fennel can be grown in cool spring weather and planted again in middle to late summer for a fall harvest.

Keep the plants evenly moist throughout the growing season; mulching is a good strategy. I have found fennel to be a very heavy feeder, so even if you have rich soil, feed the fennel every three weeks throughout the growing period with a good all-purpose fertilizer or every two weeks with a solution of fish emulsion. It takes from 80 to 90 days for the bulbs to become solid and firm; when they are ready, cut them off at soil level.

RECOMMENDED VARIETIES

Days to maturity are counted from the time of planting seed.

'TRIESTE'—90 days; French hybrid bred for large rounded bulbs with crunchy succulent flesh and sweet anise flavor; great raw in salads or cooked.

'ZEFA FINO'—65 days; from Florence; large tender anise-flavored bulb forms at base of leaf stalk.

EATING FENNEL

Now you are ready to enjoy fennel's many delights. Bulbing fennel has a texture much like celery but with a nutty, mild anise flavor. If you are eating the fennel raw, remove the first heavy wrapping layers or destring them as you would celery. Trim off the feathery leaves to use as garnish. The raw flesh is thick and crisp when slivered, sliced, or coarsely chopped. Add it to any mixed vegetable or green salad, or partner it with fresh ripe tomatoes and arugula. It is also delicious with sliced oranges and curly endive. As an appetizer, serve slivered fennel with mild soft goat cheese, olives, and shaved nutty Asiago or Parmesan cheese. Or serve thin slices of fennel for dessert, plated with cream cheese and fresh figs.

This delicious vegetable deepens and mellows when cooked, becoming sweet and succulent with a rich flavor that enhances vegetable, meat, poultry, pasta, and fish dishes. Brushed with olive oil and grilled, fennel makes a great side dish for grilled fish, especially salmon. Roast quartered fennel bulbs with chicken or with pork and apples for a meltingly delicious combination of flavors. To braise fennel, sprinkle sliced bulbs with good virgin olive oil, bake until tender, then finish with freshly grated Parmesan cheese and a few finely chopped anchovies and brown under the broiler.

Opposite: Not to be confused with the herb fennel, the vegetable fennel forms a deliciously crunchy bulblike base of overlapping stems just above soil level.

GARLIC
Allium sativum
SUSAN BELSINGER

I would have to say that out of all the vegetable crops that I cultivate, garlic is my favorite. Just the fact that planting a single clove of garlic results in a whole bulb of cloves about six months later is magical. In the fall, when days are shorter and the chill of winter is in the air, many gardeners feel a bit melancholy as they put their gardens to rest. But not the gardener who grows garlic, because that is the time of year it is planted.

GROWING GARLIC

The best time for planting garlic can vary from mid-September to early December, depending on where you live. Wait until soil temperatures are around 60°F and the first hard frost is six to eight weeks away to prepare the garlic bed. Turn the soil over and add compost, aged manure, or leaves. I usually plant four 50-foot rows, which seems like a lot for a family of four, but I always use up my garlic before the next crop comes in. I peel some of the excess papery skin off of the bulbs, breaking them apart with the heels of my hands to separate the cloves. Then I plant each clove by hand, sticking it down in the

Depending on the climate, garlic is planted between September and December and harvested the following summer. Above is 'Spanish Roja', an heirloom variety.

SUN-DRIED TOMATO, GORGONZOLA, AND ROASTED GARLIC SAUCE

Generous pound of pasta, pappardelle or fettuccine
2 cups half-and-half
1 cup crumbled gorgonzola or blue cheese
$^2/_3$ cup sun-dried tomatoes, sliced, with a little of the oil
4 heads roasted garlic, separated into cloves
2-inch sprig fresh rosemary
Salt and freshly ground black pepper
$^1/_3$ cup toasted and coarsely chopped walnuts (optional)

Put the pasta water on to boil. Pour the half-and-half into a large skillet. Add the cheese, tomatoes, garlic, and rosemary. Place over low flame and gently heat until barely simmering and cheese has melted, stirring occasionally; about 10 minutes. Add salt and pepper to taste.

Add salt to the boiling water and cook the pasta al dente. Drain the pasta and add it to the skillet. Toss the pasta with the sauce, remove the rosemary sprig, and transfer to warmed bowls. Garnish with the walnuts, if desired, and a little fresh pepper. Serve immediately. Serves six.

If you roast the garlic ahead of time (wrap each bulb tightly in aluminum foil and place in the oven for 30 minutes at 300°F), you can prepare this rich, tasty sauce in the time it takes for the pasta water to boil and the pasta to cook.

earth with my finger so that it is covered with about 1½-inches of soil. I plant the cloves about six inches apart, with the root end down, then spread straw mulch over the bed to keep weeds out.

If the weather is warm, sometimes the little cloves sprout in the fall, but it doesn't seem to deter new growth in the spring: It is always a joyous sight to see the grass-green sprouts lined up in a row. And it's delightful to eat garlic leaves when they are about 10 or 12 inches tall. Used raw in salads, pounded with a mortar and pestle to make green garlic mayonnaise, or sautéed in just a little olive oil are only a few ways to savor this gourmet treat. Sometimes I pull the bulbs before they are mature to note the swell of the bulb and to see if I can observe the forming of the individual cloves. Garlic is pungent and delicious to eat at this stage, too.

Fertilize garlic every three or four weeks during the growing season until about two weeks before the harvest. I use liquid kelp or fish emulsion. My anticipation grows when the first garlic greens start to turn brown and fall over. Generally I harvest garlic somewhere around the beginning of July (in my Zone 7 garden), or when about half or more of the tops have turned brown and fallen over. I pay attention to the weather forecast and dig up the garlic when there will be some days without rain. Do not pull up garlic. If you pull a softneck garlic at this stage, most likely the stem will separate from the bulb. I dig each bulb and lay it on the straw mulch to dry out a bit. Once all the garlic has been dug, I move it over to a deck that's in partial shade. I spend quite a bit of time brushing the soil from the bulbs and roots. Then I lay all the garlic on large screens or boards, keeping the bulbs separate to allow them to cure. The papery skins that enclose each clove and the whole bulb are damp when harvested and need about two weeks of dry weather to lose enough moisture to be ready for storage. Good air circulation speeds up the process. If it is going to rain or if heavy dew coats the ground, cover the garlic. I move mine inside a shed when the weather turns bad, but it's fine to protect the bulbs with a tarp. Once the garlic is dry, trim the roots and stems, and then store the bulbs in mesh bags. The more handsome bulbs can be braided together if they have some stem attached.

Although my garlic bulbs may not be as large as those that are commercially grown, the flavor and pungency are superior. Bringing in the garlic harvest makes me feel wealthy in many ways. These bulbs are full of vitamins and nutrients, which keep my family and friends healthy throughout the year, and they give wonderful flavor to the foods I prepare. And I also save some bulbs to plant as part of next year's crop.

RECOMMENDED VARIETIES

There are more than 300 varieties of garlic to grow; listed below are a few of my favorites. The papery outer coverings on most garlic bulbs are white, even though quite a few have red or purple tinges, mottling, or stripes. And even when the outer skin of a bulb is white, once peeled, the coverings of the garlic cloves themselves may vary in color, ranging from red, pink, and purple to brown or yellow. Garlic takes between six and seven months from planting to harvest. Varieties are usually described as early, mid-, or late season.

HARDNECK BULBS

'GERMAN EXTRA-HARDY'—Mid- to late-season harvest; stores well; cloves have red-purple skin; one of the best for winter hardiness.

'RUSSIAN RED'—Mid-season harvest; medium-size bulbs; striped outer skin and robust flavor; good winter hardiness.

'SPANISH ROJA'—Mid-season harvest; heirloom; cloves have purplish skin; better in cool than mild climates.

SOFTNECK BULBS

'INCHELIUM RED'—Mid-season harvest; light purple blotching on the papery outer covering; mild but delicious; stores well.

'EARLY ITALIAN'—Early-season harvest; pungent flavor; good for braiding.

'LATE ITALIAN'—Mid-season; pungent flavor; good storage; good for braiding.

'SILVER ROSE'—Late maturing; silver-white covering; rose-colored cloves; keeps well; good for braiding.

SHALLOTS

Allium cepa var. *aggregatum*

Shallots are good for sauces and vinaigrettes.

Fall-planted shallots are cultivated in much the same way as garlic. Plant the bulbs in loamy soil, six to eight inches apart, and fertilize every three to four weeks during the season. Shallots are also harvested when their tops start to brown and fall over. If left in the ground, they overwinter and begin to grow and divide the next spring. They share this feature with their very close relative the potato onion (*A. cepa* Aggregatum Group). Perennial potato onions are more rounded in shape, and their leaves grow together in one sheaf, similar to garlic. There are red, yellow, and white cultivars of both shallots and potato onions. The main difference is in the flavor. Shallots have a more complex flavor, particularly the teardrop-shaped types such as 'French Gray', and are less pungent than potato onions.

RECOMMENDED VARIETIES

You can start harvesting shallots about 80 days after the bulbs were planted and continue until their tops are brown and wilted, which may take anywhere from 100 to 120 days.

'DUTCH YELLOW'—Dutch; yellow skin and white flesh; pungent flavor; good keeper.

'FRENCH GRAY'—Considered the ultimate by French chefs; more elongated bulb; has a tannish skin that is thicker than other shallots, which seems to prolong its shelf life a bit; pale-colored flesh.

'GOLDEN GEMET'—French; yellow skin and white flesh; grows fairly big and round; keeps well.

'HOLLAND RED'—Forms good-sized, round, red-fleshed bulbs; flavorful but mellow; excellent keeper.

'RED GEMET'—French; produces good yield of red-fleshed bulbs; very flavorful.

'RED SUN'—French; forms round bulbs with gold skin and pink to red flesh; good flavor.

OKRA
Abelmoschus esculentus
ELIZABETH BURGER

Like many other people, when I think of okra, I think of slime. Were it not for my food-adventuring daughter, Eva, I never would have changed my mind about the tasteless, slimy creature I had once eaten as a child. Yuck.

But Eva came back from a visit to a Caribbean restaurant rhapsodizing about this vegetable with the bad name. "No, no, it's really good. It's not slimy at all," she kept saying. And so, trusting her impeccable palate, I made a leap of faith and decided to grow it in my Maryland garden. I found several varieties in my seed catalog, which assured me that okra was easy to grow, requiring warm, humid weather and full sun. In other words, it's a southern crop, perfect for Maryland.

Originally from India or Africa, the plants have been found growing wild along the banks of the White Nile. The actual name "okra" comes from West Africa, from the Ashanti word *nkruma*. Brought to North America by slaves, okra is also a favorite in South America, the Caribbean, Sri Lanka, India, and the Middle East.

GROWING OKRA

I prepare my okra bed with aged manure from the neighbor's cows, plant the seeds about an inch deep, and in about ten days, the first little leaves pop up. If you live in a cooler area, start seeds indoors four to six weeks before the last spring frost date, in individual cells or pots, three seeds to a pot. Do not use flats, because okra does not like to have its roots disturbed. Use a heating mat, and keep soil temperatures warm, from 80°F to 90°F, until plants emerge. Then provide artificial light for 14 to 16 hours every day. Transplant the seedlings to a sunny spot

Okra 'Burgundy' not only tastes good but is also a beautiful ornamental for the flower garden.

BHENDI KARI

1 pound okra
1 tbsp. ghee or oil
1 large onion, thinly sliced
2 fresh green chiles, slit open and seeded
1 clove garlic, finely sliced
$^1/_2$ tsp. fresh ginger, finely grated
$^1/_2$ tsp. ground turmeric
$^1/_2$ tsp. ground coriander
$^1/_2$ tsp. ground cumin
$1^1/_2$ cups coconut milk or buttermilk
1 tsp. salt

Wash okra, pat dry, and cut off stem ends with a sharp knife. If the pods are large, cut into convenient lengths. Heat the ghee or oil in a saucepan and sauté the onion and chiles over medium-low heat, stirring occasionally, until onions are golden. Add garlic, ginger, and turmeric and sauté, stirring, for a minute longer, then add okra and cook for three to four minutes. Add the coriander, cumin, coconut milk or buttermilk, and salt. Simmer uncovered until okra is tender, 10 to 12 minutes. Serve hot with rice. Serves four.

in the garden at about the same time you plant corn and beans, spacing them 12 to 18 inches apart. Mulch with hay and cover with floating fabric to provide additional heat early in the season.

Okra not only tastes good but is also quite ornamental. The first true leaves are deeply lobed and proceed to unfurl on a sturdy stalk that grows to about three feet before the first funnel-shaped flowers open. The exquisite ivory petals are a rosy maroon at the base, with soft yellow stamens. After the flowers, the soft green, tapering, slightly ridged seedpods appear, pointing their slender tips upward. In fact, okra has become the most popular plant in my garden. (King Louis XIV, I have read, took the same pleasure in okra in his garden at Versailles.) Occasionally, this underrated vegetable may get downy mildew, but you can avoid further infection by planting in a different location each year.

RECOMMENDED VARIETIES

'BURGUNDY'—60 days; hybrid; plant can grow to four feet in the South, only two to three feet in the North; green leaves with burgundy midribs; deep red pods; pick pods at six to eight inches.

'CAJUN DELIGHT'—55 days; hybrid; dark green spineless pods; pods grow to five inches long; harvest at three to four inches.

'COWHORN'—55 days; heirloom; plant can reach eight feet; pods grow up to 14 inches long, but pick at 5 to 6 inches long; heavy yield; gorgeous plant.

Its mucilaginous character makes okra a good base for stews and soups.

'JADE'—55 days; plant can grow to 4½ feet tall; dark green pods, tender until six inches long; high yield.

Days to maturity are counted from the time of planting seed.

EATING OKRA

A member of the mallow and hibiscus family, Malvaceae, and a relative of the cotton plant, okra is valued for its mucilaginous character, which makes the plant a good base for stews and soups. Containing protein, folic acid, fiber, calcium, magnesium, vitamin C, iron, and potassium, it is a very nutritious food source. The seeds can also be roasted and used as a coffee substitute.

If you want baby gourmet treats, pluck the furry pods when they are three to four inches long; longer pods tend to be fibrous and tough. The sculptor in me likes to see them longer, so I let a few grow larger to use in my work. I have seen them in dried arrangements, and the seeds make a pleasant rattling sound.

Many okra recipes include green chiles and onions, which enhance the subtle flavor of the vegetable. My favorite so far is an Indian preparation called *Bhendi Kari* (see recipe on page 63), which has a base of coconut milk flavored with cumin, coriander, and fresh ginger. It's true that okra can be somewhat slimy, but that's desirable for a gumbo or stew. Since it is contact with water that brings out this quality, you can minimize it by patting the okra pods dry after washing them. Then slice them into bite-size pieces. Okra's tropical origins render it particularly compatible with other hot-weather vegetables, such as tomatoes, eggplants, and peppers. Sautéed in oil with onions and peppers and lightly seasoned, the pods are succulent and sweet.

My daughter, Eva, who has been spending a few months in Senegal, called to tell me that people there use the flower to flavor a drink. I suppose I'll have to try that next year.

ONIONS, SCALLIONS, AND LEEKS
Allium species
SUSAN BELSINGER

Edible alliums, such as onions, scallions, and leeks, as well as garlic and shallots (see page 58) are featured in every cuisine throughout the world. They are used raw in salads, on sandwiches, in relishes, and more, and of course they can be fried, grilled, sautéed, boiled, roasted, or baked. They play a supporting role in countless sauces, soups, sautés, stews, and casseroles, their pungency turning savory sweet. Since all alliums contain sugars and sulfur compounds (more than 100 complex sulfur compounds found in onions are still being studied), they quickly burn or overcook and turn acrid. So cook them over medium heat, turning frequently.

GROWING ONIONS, SCALLIONS, AND LEEKS

All alliums have very shallow root systems and require fertile, well-drained, and well-worked soil. If you don't have loamy soil in your garden, add very liberal amounts of compost or well-rotted manure. For best results, add all soil amendments two or three months before sowing seed or setting out plants.

Only a few varieties of onions, scallions, and leeks are available as plants or sets; for a much wider selection, start them from seed. Fill flats with a moistened soilless growing medium that is a combination of one part sphagnum peat moss or composted bark and one part vermiculite or perlite, and sow seed thinly in rows. When the seedlings are three to four inches tall, transplant them into the garden if there is no danger of frost. If it's too early to plant them out, transplant single plants into cells to hold them over until it's warm enough outside.

Even after the onions, scallions, and leeks are growing vigorously, keep them well weeded and watered and fertilize them lightly every three

Edible alliums, such as onion, garlic, and chives, are kitchen staples all over the world.

All alliums have shallow root systems and require fertile, well-drained, and well-worked soil. Above is 'Mambo', a red variety of *Allium cepa*, bulb onion.

weeks with a kelp or fish emulsion. Onions and leeks make their best foliage and feeder-root growth during the cool, wet seasons, so make sure they have plenty of water to keep them cool and soaking up nutrients. Early growth, whether in fall or spring, is directly related to how large and well-formed onions will be at harvest.

SCALLIONS
Allium fistulosum

Depending on where you live, scallions may also be called green onions. Seed catalogs may list *A. fistulosum* as bunching onions or bulbless Japanese, Chinese, or Welsh onions. Cultivars of common onion (*Allium cepa*) are often sold as bunching onions, meant to be harvested when they're about scallion size. Set the plants out in early spring for a spring or early-summer harvest or in late summer for a fall crop. Start harvesting scallions when they are barely pencil-thin and continue digging as needed, as they're best eaten fresh. Use a trowel to harvest; they break off rather easily in any but the most friable soil. Scallions are quite frost-tender, so listen to the weather forecast and be sure to harvest them all in good time.

RECOMMENDED VARIETIES OF SCALLIONS

'RED BARON'—65 days; red from bottom of leaves to roots; plant for spring to summer harvest.

Not all onions are suited for storage. *Allium cepa* 'Copra', which is high in sulfur and low in water, keeps very well.

'SANTA CLAUS'—60 days; deep rose-red scallion; harvest in spring to summer.

'ISHIKURA'—65 days; spring or fall planting; holds well in the ground.

'EVERGREEN HARDY WHITE'—65 days; white; spring or fall planting.

'PACIFIC PEARL'—60 days; white; plant at any time of year.

'GUARDSMAN'—60 days; early when planted in spring; grows tall and strong.

LEEKS
Allium porrum

In short-season climates, sow seeds in flats at the end of February or in early March, otherwise you can sow the seed directly in the garden in late April to early May. Sow seed in rows about four to the inch. When the seedlings are four inches tall, transplant them to shallow trenches, one to two inches deep, setting them about four inches apart. (The thinnings of pencil-sized leeks are tasty uncooked in green or vegetable salads, and thumb-size leeks are excellent when cooked for salads.) It's best to grow leeks in rows, as they need to be blanched over time: As the leeks grow, gradually fill in the trenches and hill soil above ground. Harvesting leeks is a matter of choosing what size you like to eat them. Most leeks are so cold-hardy that you can leave them in the ground and continue harvesting through the winter. Just check every few weeks to make sure that they aren't getting too big and tough—one inch in diameter is probably about as thick as you want them, unless you grow one of the giant varieties.

Most leeks are so cold-hardy that you can leave them in the ground and harvest through the winter.

'BLEU SOLAISE'—100 to 120 days; hardy; beautiful shade of blue-gray foliage; medium-size and sweet.

'EMERALD ISLE'—100 days; hardy; bright green leaves; medium-size and sweet.

'GIANT MUSSELBURG'—80 to 150 days; the largest, nearly three inches in diameter.

'KING RICHARD'—75 to 80 days; the earliest to mature; very tall.

'LAURA'—115 days; hardy; can be planted in late fall to overwinter.

BULB ONIONS
Allium cepa

Bulb onions include storage onions like the pungent yellow, white, and red onions we buy at the grocery store, pearl onions, boiling onions, sweet onions, fresh onions, and cipolline, the small flat onions that Italians like to pickle. Pearl onions and boiling onions can be grown from any variety of bulb onion; plant them very thickly and harvest when they reach the desired size, between half an inch and two inches in diameter. Sweet onions are usually grown in the places they are named after, such as Walla Walla, Washington; Vidalia, Georgia; and Texas. Fresh onions are fairly high in water and low in sulfur, which means they taste sweet but don't store well.

Day length is the most critical factor for producing bulb onions: Long-day onions require long hours of daylight (14 hours or more) to set off bulb formation, conditions found at latitudes above 40 degrees. Intermediate-day onions are grown in regions that have about equal hours of daylight and darkness during the late spring and early summer, conditions found at between 32 and 40 degrees latitude. Short-day types need less daylight and grow successfully only at latitudes of 32 degrees or lower.

Long-day onions are sown in the ground as early as the weather permits in spring or, more commonly, started in flats in winter to set out in early spring. Intermediate-day types can be sown in the spring or started in the fall for a late-spring or early-summer harvest. Short-day cultivars are always sown outdoors in fall for early-spring to early-summer harvest.

Most onions take between 75 and 120 days to reach maturity but can be pulled at any time to eat. Many gardeners sow them close together so that they can eat the thinnings. When between 25 percent and 50 percent of the onion tops have fallen naturally, most growers recommend pushing over the remaining tops. It makes sense to do this gently, with your hands or the back of a rake, to minimize damage to the necks of the plants. Withhold water for about a week to begin the curing process in the ground. The plants need at least five days of exposure to the heat and light of the sun; if it rains, cover the onions and begin the curing again. Remove the onions from the ground before the tops rot; they should be limp and may be green or dry.

Finish curing the onions by spreading them in one layer on screens, or anything else that allows good air circulation. In hot, sunny weather they will cure in about a week. During cool, cloudy weather they may need up to two weeks. Protect the onions from any dampness, whether from rain or dew. The neck, where the top meets the bulb, is the most important part of the onion to be cured and dried, since it is the point where molds enter the bulb. Separate thick- and thin-necked onions and use the thick-necked ones first; thin-necked onions store best.

Once cured, onions may be stored in braids or with their tops clipped. If you clip the tops, leave one- to two-inch stubs to dry completely.

RECOMMENDED VARIETIES OF BULB ONIONS

LONG-DAY VARIETIES

'BORETTANA'—80 days; Italian heirloom; cipolline, small flat pickling onions.

'AILSA CRAIG'—100 to 110 days; yellow onion of moderate pungency; forms good-sized bulb; easy to grow; good keeper.

'COPRA'—105 days; firm, yellow; ideal for storage.

'WALLA WALLA'—125 days if spring-sown, 300 days if summer-sown and overwintered; Washington State version of 'Vidalia'; sweet; stores for a month or two.

'RED BURGENMASTER'—100 days; large red- and white-ringed bulbs; good flavor.

'NEW YORK'—100 days; yellow; medium storage.

INTERMEDIATE-DAY VARIETIES

'CANDY'—135 days; day-neutral; yellow; pungent yet sweet; good for storage.

'SUPER STAR'—110 days; day-neutral; large white bulbs; not a great keeper.

'ITALIAN TORPEDO'—110 days; red; known for its elongated bottle shape.

'RED WETHERSFIELD'—115 days; big red bulbs; good flavor.

'BLANCO DURO'—120 days; white; not a great keeper.

SHORT-DAY VARIETIES

'TEXAS SWEET 1015'—105 days; sweet and mild; stores only for a month or two.

'VIDALIA' OR 'GRANEX SWEET'—150 days; famous southern sweet onion; flattish bulb; short storage.

PEAS
Pisum sativum
LEE REICH

In some circles, a gardener's skill is measured by how soon he or she gets the first mess of shelling peas on the dinner table. Peas are a good choice for such a competition because raising a good crop demands the best soil you can muster, as well as timely sowing and harvesting. Peas are a cool-weather crop (50°F to 70°F is best), so they must be planted early: Not too early, though, or the seeds are apt to rot; not too late, either, for the plants languish in hot weather.

Beyond the competitive edge, striving for the earliest possible crop of shelling peas is also a worthy goal because peas are the quintessential garden delicacy. The sugars in peas start changing to starches just as soon as the pods are picked, so it is impossible to buy fresh, frozen, or canned peas that match the flavor of just-harvested homegrown ones.

I'll admit to being drawn into the spirit of pea competition, albeit with some reservations. I won't grow smooth-seeded shelling peas, such as 'Alaska', which are the earliest. They don't taste as good as wrinkle-seeded types, whose seeds wrinkle up because they are so high in sugar. I won't use fungicide-treated seeds, which can be planted earlier with less danger of rotting. Handling poison-coated seeds takes the fun out of pea planting. And as quantity is also important to me, I would never start peas indoors in pots because it would be impossible to manage enough transplants to get a decent meal.

GROWING PEAS

Pondering the question of when to drop those first seeds into furrows, too many gardeners bow to tradition and sow them—or try to—on St. Patrick's Day, March 17. St. Patrick's Day may be the ideal date for planting peas in Ireland, but sometime in January is more on the mark in Florida; or sometime in May in Minnesota. Here in New York, I plant peas on April 1, which is seven weeks before the average date of our last killing frost. Pea seeds germinate as long as the soil temperature is above 40°F, so you could stay on top of the vagaries of the season by sticking a thermometer into the soil to find out exactly when the soil hits that temperature in spring. Or watch for forsythia blossoms, which begin to unfold at about the same time.

No matter when peas are planted, there are some tricks that help get the sprouts up more quickly and growing vigorously. Presprouting the seeds indoors gives them a slight jump on the season once they're in the ground, and planting less deeply than recommended, or in raised beds, gives them warmer soil, which also speeds sprouting and growth. Take note, though: Dramatic efforts at getting peas going will not translate into equally dramatic early har-

Opposite: Peas are a cool-weather crop and must be planted early in the growing season. Snow pea 'Oregon Sugar Pod' produces a large crop of big, tasty pods.

vests, since the plants grow slowly in the early, cool part of the season. If you've never grown peas in your garden, sprinkle the seeds with a bacterial inoculant that helps legumes, such as peas, make use of atmospheric nitrogen.

It's also important to space the plants properly. Rather than planting in single rows, sow double rows about six inches apart, with two inches between peas in a row. It's also helpful to prop the vines up off the ground. Peas reign as king in British vegetable gardens, where they are traditionally staked with pea twigs— tree and shrub prunings trimmed so that their branches lie in one plane, then pushed into the soil between each double row, with their butt ends down and branches fanned out down the row. Even before the vines start their ascent, the row of pea twigs can be attractive. I forego the twigs with a temporary fence of chicken wire, which is easier to erect. Dwarf varieties and so-called afila types, which have tendrils instead of leaves, can support themselves in a double row or mass planting without any trellis. Then again, staying short or growing less leaf area makes for lower yields.

Planting practices for snap peas and snow peas are the same as for shelling peas. The only difference is when to harvest. Harvest snap peas when the pods are fully plump and snow peas while the peas are just starting to bulge within the pods but the pods are still flat.

Among wrinkle-seeded shelling peas, you'll find some, but not many, differences in flavor from one variety to the next. Therefore, consider each variety's vine size, which determines how big a trellis you need, and days to maturity. If I have to reach to pick a pod, I want it to be stuffed with as many peas as possible. But no matter what the variety, timely harvest—which may mean every other day, or more often in hot weather—is all-important for best quality. Harvest while the pods are plump and still a vibrant green.

RECOMMENDED VARIETIES

Days to maturity are counted from the time of planting seed.

WRINKLE-SEEDED SHELLING PEAS
'DAYBREAK'—53 days; vine size 28 inches; good early variety.
'GREEN ARROW'—67 days; vine size 36 inches.
'LINCOLN'—65 days; vine size 36 inches.
'TALL TELEPHONE'—70 days; vine size 60 inches; good yield; late crop; good heat tolerance.

SNAP PEAS
'SUGAR SNAP'—62 days; vine size 60 inches; very tasty large pods; keeps producing into hot weather.
'SUGAR SPRINT'—58 days; vine size 24 inches; good flavor and almost stringless.

SNOW PEAS
'OREGON GIANT'—60 days; vine size 30 inches; large and very sweet pods.
'OREGON SUGAR POD'—68 days; vine size 28 inches; large, long pods; good yields; good for freezing.

Sugars in peas start changing to starches just as soon as the pods are harvested, so it's impossible to buy peas that match the flavor of fresh-picked homegrown ones.

EATING PEAS

If shelling peas have one fault, compared with snap peas or snow peas, it is the time it takes to shell them. In the interest of science, I once decided to quantify the actual time involved. To my surprise, I was able to pop open about six quarts of pods to make two quarts of shelled peas in only 30 minutes. Not bad, really, when it's June and you're sitting outside in the shade with a warm breeze caressing your back.

In all honesty, I consider shelling peas so delectable a treat that I eat them fresh out of the pod in season and steamed, straight from the freezer, the rest of the year. I suppose a dab of butter wouldn't hurt the flavor of the steamed ones.

PEPPERS
Capsicum annuum
SUSAN BELSINGER

Peppers are just as important in my summer garden as tomatoes and basil. In fact, while I usually germinate about a dozen different types of tomatoes and basil, I cultivate at least 20 varieties of peppers. A professed chile-head, I usually germinate at least a dozen or more kinds of chile peppers alone. They are different from the sweet peppers because they contain capsaicin, which makes them so pungent and hot.

GROWING PEPPERS

The first thing to consider when growing peppers is space. Each plant needs two to three feet of space around it, depending on variety; full sunlight; and good soil. Chiles are good container plants provided the pots are large enough; small

Experimenting with different varieties of chile peppers allows you to adjust the heat of any dish. Above are slightly hot ancho peppers.

ornamentals, for example, can be grown in five-gallon pots. The big peppers—bells, Anaheim, New Mexican, pasilla, poblano, and mulato—are produced on large plants, which usually need staking as well as space to grow without competition. Medium-size peppers—paprika, banana, cherry pepper, jalapeño, and serrano—grow on smaller bushes but often need some support as well.

I start seeds in a premixed sterile, soilless medium that is one part perlite or vermiculite to one part spaghnum peat moss. Wet the mix and spread it in sterile flats or single-cell planting trays. Sow the seeds in rows in flats, or put two seeds into each cell in planting trays. Cover the seeds lightly with about ⅛-inch of mix, and spray or mist with water. Cover the flats or trays with plastic wrap and place them in a warm

PEPERONATA

3 large sweet bell peppers: 1 red, 1 yellow, and 1 green
3 tbsp. olive oil
1 small onion, sliced lengthwise in $^1/_4$-inch slivers
2 to 3 garlic cloves, slivered
1 large tomato, diced (optional)
Leaves from 1 or 2 oregano and/or marjoram sprigs or a scant teaspoon
of dried leaves, crumbled
Salt and freshly ground pepper

Wash the peppers, stem and seed them, and remove any large ribs. Cut them lengthwise into $^3/_8$-inch strips. Heat the olive oil in a skillet. Sauté the peppers over medium heat, stirring occasionally, for about five minutes. Add the onion and garlic and cook for about five more minutes. If using tomato, add it to the skillet. Cook for about three minutes, stirring occasionally. Add the oregano and/or marjoram and season with salt and pepper. Lower the heat, stir the ingredients, cover the pan, and cook for 10 minutes or so. Serve hot or at room temperature. Serves four to six.

There are many variations of this Italian-inspired stew. Sometimes it is made without herbs, sometimes with basil rather than marjoram or oregano, sometimes with nary a tomato. You might try adding a few tablespoons of dry red or white wine. It is a very versatile late-summer dish, colorful and always tasty. The stew tastes even better when made ahead of time. Serve it as a side vegetable, on bruschetta as an appetizer, or as a topping for pasta or pizza.

This recipe is adapted from *Herbs in the Kitchen*, by Carolyn Dille and Susan Belsinger (Interweave Press, 1992).

room. Check after a week to be sure that they are still moist; seeds germinate within one to two weeks.

As soon as the seeds germinate, remove the plastic wrap and place the flats under grow-lights suspended four to five inches above the seedlings. Any fluorescent fixture that has two tubes—one warm and one cool—works fine. Provide the seedlings with 16 hours of light a day for two weeks, and feed once a week with a fertilizer that is high in calcium nitrate.

In about two weeks, the seedlings will produce their first two sets of leaves; transplant them to small, individual-cell trays, or thin them to just one seedling if you started them in cell trays. Place the seedlings in a greenhouse or sunny window for at least two more weeks. Fertilize once a week and water as necessary. Harden pepper seedlings off for about two weeks before planting them in the garden.

Once the pepper seedlings have hardened off, set them out in the garden or plant them into large pots. Plant sweet and chile peppers in separate areas to avoid cross-pollination. Plant the peppers in rows three feet apart, with 18 to 30 inches between plants, depending on size. Peppers grow best in well-drained

Chile peppers differ from sweet peppers in that they contain capsaicin, which gives them pungency and heat. Above is 'Aji Amarillo'.

loamy soil with plenty of organic matter, such as compost or aged manure. Fertilize regularly with a solution that's high in calcium nitrate, which is important for heavy fruit and abundant yields.

In cooler climates with a short growing season, consider growing peppers and other members of the nightshade family through black plastic, as their roots will not grow when the soil temperature is below 55°F.

To promote large yields, harvest the first green peppers as soon as they are fully developed. They should be evenly colored and firm. In the right climate, with good cultivation practices and continuous harvesting, pepper production can last from one to three months after the first harvest.

RECOMMENDED VARIETIES

If left on the vine, both sweet and hot peppers will ripen from green to other colors progressively. In the list below, the first number indicates how many days it takes from transplanting the seedlings to producing mature green peppers; the second number indicates how long it takes until the peppers turn to shades of red, yellow, purple, or mahogany, depending on the variety.

SWEET BELL PEPPERS

'ACE'—50 days green/70 days red; earliest to harvest; good yield.

If left on the vine, sweet and hot peppers will ripen from green to other colors progressively. Above is a sweet pepper that turns a rich chocolate color with maturity.

'CADICE'—55 days green/75 days red; French variety; does well in cool areas; fairly early.

'RED KNIGHT'—60 days green/80 days red; blocky; thick and sweet; turns red early.

'YANKEE BELL'—60 days green/80 days red; medium-size pepper; keeps well once mature red.

'JINGLE BELLS'—50 days green/70 days red; miniature; blocky 1½ to 2-inch fruit on compact plant; similar mini bell peppers are available in chocolate and yellow.

YELLOW PEPPERS

'EARLY SUNSATION'—50 days green/70 days golden; early, thick-walled yellow fruit.

'LABRADOR'—60 days green/80 days yellow; medium-size sweet peppers; holds well on vine.

'QUADRATO ASTI GIALLO'—60 days green/80 days yellow; thick, sweet, blocky Italian variety.

OTHER COLORS

'CHOCOLATE BEAUTY' OR 'SWEET CHOCOLATE'—about 60 days green/80 days brown; medium-size fruit; good raw or cooked.

'ISLANDER'—56 days lavender-purple/80 days red; matures through a rainbow of colors, from lavender to yellow to orange to red; good raw.

'LILAC BEL'—60 days green/80 days lilac; matures from a pale green to lavender to crimson purple.

SWEET HEIRLOOM PEPPERS

'CORNO DI TORO'—50 days green/70 days red; bull's horn peppers are good green or mature red; great raw, fried, or stewed.

'MARCONI'—70 days green/90 days red, Italian heirloom; long, sweet frying pepper.

CHILE PEPPERS

ANCHOS—65 days green/85 days red; mild to slightly hot chile; heart-shaped stuffing pepper; called poblano when dried.

'BOLDOG'—60 days green/80 days red; paprika; crimson red; sweet, with just a touch of heat.

HABANEROS—75 days green/100 days yellow or red; small, lantern-shaped chiles; fruity and among the most incendiary.

'HUASTECO'—55 days green/75 days red; serrano; good hot chile heat and superior flavor; my favorite chile pepper.

'NUMEX JOE E. PARKER'—70 days green/95 days red; Anaheim type; mild heat; extra large; good for rellenos.

'PURIRA AJI'—55 days green/75 days yellow; thin-walled; very hot, with a fruity fragrance and taste; good for salsas, salads, and beans.

'SANTA FE GRANDE'—60 days yellow-green/80 days orange to red, medium and blocky in size and heat; turns from yellow to orange to scarlet as it matures.

'THAI DRAGON'—50 days green/70 days red; extremely hot; slender, small chile; very flavorful.

EATING PEPPERS

All sweet peppers are wonderful, whether used raw for salads or relishes, sautéed in summer stir-fries, stuffed and baked, grilled, or puréed into sauces. All peppers have a thin skin, which is removed by roasting and peeling. I like the robust flavor of the red paprika peppers in soups and stews and dry them in the oven to use in the winter months. The recently introduced miniature bell pepper 'Jingle Bells' is perfect for tiny stuffed peppers. A plateful of them makes a fun appetizer or first course when filled with rice, other grains, cheese, and herbs.

It's nice to experiment with different varieties of chile pepper, adjusting the heat of a dish on a whim. Sometimes I want the mild heat of a Santa Fe Grande or a jalapeño in my scrambled eggs; other times I like the assertive taste and heat of a few serranos in my salsa. I love the chile rush of a fruity habanero minced fine in my mango salsa or pot of black beans. I'm also fond of poblanos, mild to slightly hot chiles that are traditionally roasted, peeled, stuffed, and fried to make chiles rellenos, green chile sauce, or stew.

Opposite: A colorful assortment of heirloom sweet and hot peppers.

POTATOES
Solanum tuberosum
JOAN DYE GUSSOW

Visitors to my garden are often surprised that I grow potatoes, allotting them more space than I give over to that queen of vegetable fruits, the tomato. As an edible object, the potato has been popularly reduced to a box of sticks fried in fat or a foil-wrapped lump, slashed open to serve as another fat carrier. Since "garden-fresh" doesn't seem to have much meaning where potatoes are concerned, why bother producing them? Seriously growing potatoes seems, well… overserious.

For many of my vegetable-gardening years, almost 20 I'm afraid, I felt much the same about the nonessentiality of homegrown potatoes. Five or six years after my husband and I started to garden seriously, we added potatoes to our list of crops. But it was a minor adventure, a curiosity, and we grew only one kind— the brilliantly colored 'Red Norland', which were fun to unearth.

In the end, though, looks were not enough. Eventually, it sank in that we had no usable potatoes past December, and that it might be nice to try some variety that would store better. Thoughts of extended storage were prompted by my growing determination to eat locally throughout the year. In any such enterprise, potatoes would clearly need to play a major role.

I don't remember how we first learned of Ronnigers, a family company (by now twice merged) devoted almost entirely to potatoes, but their catalog initiated us into serious potato growing. There we learned of early, middle, and late

If you grow enough potato varieties that store well, such as 'Yellow Finn' above, you'll be able to enjoy homegrown tubers all winter long.

POTATOES AND PASTA WITH HERB PASTE

1 pound 'White Rose' or red potatoes
$^1/_2$ pound orecchiette or other small pasta shapes
2 tsp. fresh rosemary (or 1 tsp. dried)
12 fresh sage leaves (or 1 tsp. dried)
$^1/_4$ cup parsley
3 large garlic cloves
15 peppercorns
5 juniper berries
$^1/_2$ tsp. coarse salt
2 tbsp. virgin olive oil
$^1/_3$ cup unsalted butter

Peel the potatoes, cut into bite-size pieces, and boil until tender in a pot of salted water. Bring a second pot of water to a boil, add salt to taste, and cook pasta until al dente. Meanwhile, roughly chop the rosemary, sage, parsley, and garlic. Remove to a mortar and pound to a paste with the peppercorns, juniper berries, and salt. Put the herb-garlic mix in a bowl with the olive oil and butter. When the potatoes and pasta are done, drain them, add to the herbs, toss together, and serve immediately. Serves four.

This recipe is adapted from *The Savory Way*, by Deborah Madison, Bantam Books, 1990.

varieties, of heavy and light producers, of good keepers and bad. And we went from one variety to seven in a single bound.

The names in the catalog lured me from the beginning, speaking as they did of exotic origins and Native American traditions. Here are some I've grown after 'Red Norland': 'Garnet Chile', 'Red Lasoda', 'Yellow Finn', 'Bintje', 'Haida', 'Anoka', 'Urgenta', 'Lakota', 'Bison', 'Desirée', 'Larote', and 'Purple Peruvian'. Note that there are more than seven varieties here. They go and come only because I can't try new ones if I keep planting the varieties I've already tried. Maybe I'll try 'Dazoc' next year. "Talk about a delicious red potato!" cheers the seed catalog. "This one is an old North Dakota variety, long since disappeared from commercial markets. The flesh of most reds is useful for potato salad or steaming, but 'Dazoc' is also delicious baked and a fine hash-browner too. And 'Dazoc' stores until the new crop produces new potatoes—now that's a good keeper!" Talk about irresistible!

GROWING POTATOES

On the issue of potato yield, you'll have to trust the seed catalog. Too many things other than the variety affect yield in the garden. In the same space, I grew more than 70 pounds of potatoes one year and less than 40 another. The poor year the garden was flooded twice. But on the whole the fingerlings—the little ones—yield less than the larger ones, and the Dutch variety 'Bintje' is so productive that the Dutch apparently had to restrict planting in the Netherlands to avoid the risk of monocropping—everyone wanted to grow it.

As a contribution to the garden aesthetic, the potato is lovely—at least for a while. Above the ground, it grows a nice-looking plant with a somewhat tomato-like leaf and pretty white or lilac or subtly pink or blue flowers, while down below it's storing up starch in the tubers we like to eat.

For years, I've grown potatoes in the ground like most folks, starting with a soil that I do my best to make "deep, light, and loose"—that perfect soil everyone yearns for. Mostly I put in as much compost as I have to spare, add a well-rounded organic fertilizer, and avoid lime because potatoes come out cleanest in a slightly acidic soil.

You can try starting potatoes quite early, several weeks before the last frost, but seed potatoes really prefer soil that's warmer than 55°F, and they'll rot if it's too cold, so don't press your luck. (I've been trying lately to grow potatoes in wire bins above the ground because I have flooding problems. But success has been intermittent, so I wouldn't advise it for a beginner.)

When I'm ready to plant in my three-foot-wide beds, I pull soil away from the center to make a trench six to eight inches deep, in which I space the seed potatoes 10 to 15 inches apart. (A "seed potato" is a small potato or a small piece of a larger potato cut so that each piece has at least one "eye" from which the potato plant can sprout.) I then cover with a little soil, and as the shoots grow, I hill the soil up around them, because the potatoes form above the "seed." Then I chop up oak leaves and keep heaping them around the plants as they grow, to give the crop even more space and to keep away potato beetles—I think. At least those ugly red larvae have never bothered my oak-mulched potatoes. As an added benefit, the oak leaves get dug into the soil when you harvest the potatoes, adding organic matter for next year's crop. (Something other than potatoes, I hope. They shouldn't be put in the same ground two years in a row.)

You'll know the plants are making tubers when they bloom. That's when some gardeners sneak their hands in and "steal" a young potato because they can't wait. When the plants die down, usually in July and August, it's a signal to dig them—one of my favorite gardening activities. Note where the stems emerge from the ground, and, at least eight inches away, gently (!) sink a turning fork full into the soil and pull back. If you've done your job right, you should unearth lots of potatoes. Let them dry off, brush off dirt, and store them in ventilated boxes or bags (I actually wash them gently and let them thoroughly dry on newspaper before I put them away). Remove any rotting or damaged tubers for immediate eating and store the rest in a cool, dark place.

RECOMMENDED VARIETIES

Days to maturity are counted from the time the seed potatoes are planted.

'BINTJE'—90 plus days; a prodigious producer; nice-looking potato.

'FRENCH FINGERLING'—90 plus days; a lovely small, reddish-skinned potato with yellowish flesh. Better-yielding for me than most of the fingerlings.

'PURPLE PERUVIAN'—90 plus days; absolutely indomitable; comes up next year even if you dig them all; stores well; tolerates everything because life is tough in the Andes, where it comes from.

'RED NORLAND'—65 plus days; a beautiful red potato; quick to sprout in storage but high-yielding for me.

'SANGRE'—80 plus days; a red potato that's no beauty but tasty and a great keeper.

'YELLOW FINN'—90 plus days; the best-yielding of the yellows for me; delicious.

EATING POTATOES

As is the case with other fruits and vegetables I grow, the general deliciousness of the product and my delight at getting a big enough crop to take me through the year overwhelm my ability to make subtle distinctions between their flavors. Homegrown potatoes are homegrown potatoes, and they're just different. They're almost always smaller than the standard store potato, variously colored, and some-

times smoother or lumpier or more eyed. And it seems to be true that the reds are lower in starch—good for potato salad but poor mashers.

I'm learning to tell them apart—I'd know a 'French Fingerling' anywhere—but I don't always keep them separate when I'm cooking. The very smallest ones of any variety, less than an inch in diameter, get captured and put into a box labeled Tiny Taters. They're generally red, white (well, beige, really), and blue, and whoever gets to eat with me when I steam them up and dress them with butter and Parmesan cheese is privileged, because it happens only once a year! Any one of the varieties I grow is absolutely delicious steamed either whole or cut up and then rolled around in a pan where a bit of minced garlic has frizzled in butter.

Resilient in the garden and excellent for storage, 'Purple Peruvian' originated in the Andes.

83

SALAD GREENS

ELLEN OGDEN

Lettuce, the queen of the salad bowl, is an ideal crop for intensive vegetable gardening. It grows fast, is adaptable to different seasons, and is tolerant of most conditions. At our seed trial and display gardens in Burlington, Vermont, we complement our lettuce patch with close to 40 varieties of unusual salad greens. Some are wild, others are cultivated. All provide a range of flavors, leaf forms, and colors to a basic green salad.

We began growing gourmet salad greens in the early 1980s, always on the lookout for tasty varieties that would accommodate our Zone 3 climate. We had a farm stand, and lettuces were just about the only crop we could start early enough to have a harvest by the time we opened for business in May. Mesclun hadn't been introduced to the supermarkets yet, and we began growing a range of different salad greens and making up our own. (The word "mesclun" originated in Europe; it essentially means a mixture of cultivated greens and those gathered wild in the field.)

Seeds for these more exotic greens originally came to us as gifts from friends and neighbors. They returned home from trips to Europe with seeds for greens that they had eaten in a salad, hoping we'd re-create the experience for them.

Fast-growing, adaptable to different seasons, and tolerant of most conditions, lettuce varieties are great for experimenting in the vegetable garden.

After studying the pictures on the packets and listening to our friends' descriptions, we'd sow the seeds, mark the spot, and water. Eventually we began to import seeds by the kilo—enough to plant larger sections of the garden and meet growing customer demand.

GROWING SALAD GREENS

Greens are one of the most satisfying vegetables to grow, since they usually pop up out of the ground less than a week after sowing. And luckily, most greens will tolerate just about any kind of weather. Spring and fall are the natural seasons for good greens, but you can produce good crops right through the summer in all but the hottest climates by using a few tricks we've learned over the years.

To germinate cool-weather greens such as arugula, mâche, and most types of lettuce during hot weather, sow the seed, water well, and then cover the rows with a board to keep the seed cool until it germinates. During early and late summer, when a little shade is enough, we plant our greens in beds between the rows of beans or peas, which run north-south in our garden; this gives the more heat-sensitive plants partial shade for most of the day. During the real dog days, we put hoops of fence wire over the beds of greens and cover them with nylon shade cloth. We can grow most greens right through the summer this way.

Not readily available commercially, mâche, or corn salad, is a mild yet very tasty salad green.

Finding space to grow 40 types of salad greens may be a challenge in a home garden. Luckily, premixed mesclun seed comes to the rescue for small-space gardeners, combining loose-leafed lettuces, chicories, and other bitter or tart greens in precise proportions.

The downside of premixed mesclun is that the end product is not as well blended as one would hope, as different greens inevitably grow at different rates. Sowing seeds for a variety of greens in separate patches and blending them together after the harvest is ideal. It is the best way to regulate how much seed to grow and to coordinate the timing for a good succession of greens throughout the season. Most greens will be ready for harvest three to six weeks after they have been sown.

RECOMMENDED VARIETIES

Most salad greens and mesclun mixes are "cut and come again," which means once cut, they will resprout, yielding a second harvest in several weeks. Yet this bonus crop is not always as tender and succulent as the first growth and will often bolt and go to seed faster. The trick to continuous lettuce and salad-green production is to grow them in succession, which means sowing a new crop every two weeks. Keep going as long as you can into the fall; cold weather heightens the flavor of most salad greens.

Piquant mustard greens, such as the purple variety above, provide a nice contrast in the salad bowl, enhancing color, flavor, and texture.

TRADITIONAL MESCLUN

MISTICANZA—A Piedmontese salad mix of four lettuces and five chicories; colorful, mild lettuces combined with tart, slightly bitter greens.

NIÇOISE—A collection of once-wild greens, including dandelion, cress, and arugula, this is a spicy blend.

PROVENÇAL—Loose-leafed lettuces along with spicy chervil, peppery arugula, and tart endive.

VARIETIES OF SALAD GREENS

ARUGULA, ROCKET (*ERUCA SATIVA*)—Notched leaves resemble oak leaves; grows to five inches; can be quite spicy but easily tamed with a dressing.

BROADLEAF CRESS (*BRASSICA JUNCEA* VAR. *INTEGRIFOLIA*)—Larger leaves than plain cress; slow to bolt; leaves have a clear, peppery flavor.

CLAYTONIA, MINER'S LETTUCE, OR WINTER PURSLANE (*MONTIA PERFOLIATA*)—Young leaves are tender and form a cup-shaped rosette; tiny, white, funnel-shaped flowers look pretty in a salad or as a garnish.

CRESS (*LEPIDIUM SATIVUM*)—Tightly curled leaves like a diminutive parsley on slender stems; used to be known as "peppergrass"; excellent cut-and-come-again herb, although flavor will increase in intensity during later harvests; easy to grow; not to be confused with upland cress and watercress.

MÂCHE, OR CORN SALAD (*VALERIANELLA LOCUSTA*)—Hard to germinate; requires per-

The trick to continuous salad-green production is to grow greens in succession, which means sowing a new crop every two weeks. Above is claytonia.

A popular salad green, spicy arugula is just as welcome in soups and sautés.

fect temperatures (around 50°F) in combination with constant moisture; grows slowly; mild but very tasty spoon-shaped leaves.

MINUTINA, OR ERBA STELLA (*PLANTAGO CORYNOPSIS*)—Narrow, grasslike leaves with serrated notches and a nodding tip; mild yet assertive flavor.

MUSTARDS: 'OSAKA PURPLE' (*BRASSICA JUNCEA*), 'SOUTHERN CURLED' (*B. JUNCEA*), MIZUNA (*B. RAPA* SUBSP. *NIPPOSINICA* VAR. *LACINIATA*)—Frilly-edged leaves of deep purple; best when picked small; provides a nice contrast in a green salad.

PURSLANE 'GOLDGELBER' (*PORTULACA OLERACEA*)—Similar to wild purslane, but instead of hugging the ground, it stands upright; golden-green leaves; succulent, with a mildly acerbic flavor; high in omega-3 fatty acids.

SELVATICA (*DIPLOTAXIS ERUCOIDES*)—Possibly a wild form of arugula with smaller leaves; hardy enough to overwinter in Zone 3; heat-tolerant, slower to bolt than garden arugula.

SHUNGIKU (*CHRYSANTHEMUM CORONARIUM*)—Harvest leaves while small; plant eventually grows into a large ornamental with pale yellow flowers.

EATING SALAD GREENS

Getting to know salad greens on an individual basis takes time and garden space, but the simplicity and the pleasure of seasonal greens brings an intriguing bounty to the salad bowl. In the fall, slow-growing mâche is often ready along with a crop of baby beets. When this happens, try making a salad of mâche, boiled and sliced white or golden beets, and hard-boiled eggs dressed with walnut oil vinaigrette.

Many of the savory small-leafed greens are especially versatile. Arugula doubles as a salad green or as a seasoning in gazpacho, and it provides a welcome piquancy when chopped into a salad of lentils and couscous. For a mustardy accent, add cress to sandwiches and salad dressings. Combining various shapes and colors adds visual delight to a tasty salad of mixed greens; for example, the grassy leaves of mild minutina contrast strikingly with the more rounded lettuce leaves.

On a recent cooking-class tour in our display gardens in Burlington, participants nibbled their way through the garden, tasting claytonia, purslane, shungiku, and minutina. They inhaled the aroma of lemon and cinnamon basil, chewed borage flowers, and sampled mustard leaves.

Then we harvested our greens and made a simple vinaigrette, first lightly seasoning the wooden salad bowl by rubbing the inside with salt and crushed garlic. Into the bowl we measured four parts extra virgin olive oil to one part herbed vinegar, added the greens, and tossed. With a light dressing, mixed salad greens come alive with a burst of flavors, tantalizing with unsurpassable color and form.

SALAD DRESSING FOR WILD GREENS

1 cup olive oil
$^1/_4$ cup balsamic vinegar
3 cloves garlic, peeled and smashed
1 tbsp. fresh (or 1 tsp. dried) thyme
1 tbsp. nutritional yeast
1 tbsp. Dijon-style mustard
2 tbsp. tamari (soy sauce)
1 tbsp. honey

Place all the ingredients in a blender. Whir until completely smooth. Transfer to a bottle and store in the refrigerator. This is a very healthy dressing. The amount of nutritional yeast can vary depending on your personal tolerance and the type that you use, as some are milder than others.

Salads can be made with all kinds of wild and cultivated greens. In the Northeast, we've got plenty of sheep sorrel, purslane, dandelion, and chickweed greens growing in and around the garden. We'll add these to our salad bowl along with Johnny-jump-ups, calendula, nasturtiums, and other edible flowers.

The best way to serve a salad of tender wild greens is to toss them together in a bowl. If they need to be washed, make certain the greens are completely dry before tossing. Serve dressing alongside the salad in a pitcher with a spoon. Each person can dress his or her own salad; that way the greens will stay crisp.

SHIITAKE MUSHROOMS
Lentinula edodes
HENRY N. HOMEYER

Growing mushrooms—the phrase conjures images of dark, damp places, of rank-smelling mushroom caves filled with horse manure. But since I like cooking with mushrooms, I decided to explore the possibility of growing my own, sans the rank-smelling caves. I learned that shiitake mushrooms can be grown with a minimal amount of effort, and that once you have colonized a log with shiitake spawn, it may produce mushrooms off and on for five years.

GROWING SHIITAKE MUSHROOMS

To grow your own shiitakes, you need a supply of hardwood logs, four to six inches in diameter and four feet long. And of course you need mushroom spawn: wooden plugs—⁵⁄₁₆ of an inch in diameter and about one inch long—inoculated with the shiitake fungus. You can get 150 plugs, enough for three to four logs, for about $10. From the same companies that provide the spawn you can also order food-grade wax, which you use to seal the logs after inoculating them. You will also need a drill with a ⁵⁄₁₆-inch bit, an electric frying pan (or a hot plate and an old pot), a hammer, a paintbrush, and a shady place outdoors to store your logs. That's it. Two people working together can inoculate half a dozen logs in an hour.

What kind of logs should you get? Oak (*Quercus* species) is excellent, as is poplar (*Populus* species). Poplar logs produce mushrooms more quickly than oak; however, since their wood is softer, they deteriorate sooner and stop producing sooner. Most other hardwoods are fine, but avoid fruit trees, elm, walnut, red maple, and conifers.

If you don't have access to a chain saw and trees that can be harvested, look in the Yellow Pages under "Firewood." Explain what you are planning to do, and tell the dealer that you need freshly cut logs, not dry firewood. Ideally, you should get the freshly cut logs in the winter, since logs cut when the trees are dormant last the longest. Regardless of the time of year, it is important to buy fresh logs, because you want to avoid inoculating logs that already have fungus growing in them.

Once you have obtained your wood and spawn plugs, you are ready to inoculate the logs. First, drill a series of ⁵⁄₁₆-inch holes in the logs: Start a couple of inches from the end of the log and drill a row of holes, spacing them six to eight inches apart. Then rotate the log and drill another row of holes two inches from the first, staggering the holes so that the first one in row two is halfway between the first two holes in row one. Continue on around the log. Then hammer the spawn plugs into place. Now it's time to seal. Melt the wax—a grungy old electric frying pan set at 300°F is perfect for the job—and apply it with a cheap paintbrush.

Another way of inoculating logs has recently been introduced using "thimble spawn." The plugs are larger—thimble-size—and come embedded in a plastic

Opposite: It takes about six months to grow shiitake mushrooms from spawn on tree logs.

TUSCAN-STYLE SHIITAKE MUSHROOMS

$1/2$ pound fresh shiitake mushrooms
2 tbsp. olive oil
$1/2$ cup onion, chopped
$1/2$ cup water or broth
2 tsp. cornstarch in $1/4$ cup cold water
1 tsp. sugar
1 tsp. salt
1 tbsp. soy sauce
$1/2$ tsp. dried savory

Tear the mushrooms into bite-size pieces, removing the stems. Heat the oil in a skillet over medium heat. Add the onion and sauté until slightly browned, two or three minutes. Add the water or broth and the mushrooms and cover the skillet. Simmer for 20 minutes at low heat, stirring occasionally. In a small bowl, mix the cornstarch in water with the sugar, salt, soy sauce, and savory. Add to the mushrooms and simmer, stirring, for another five minutes. Serve on a bed of freshly cooked pasta. Serves four.

sheet. They require somewhat larger holes and are designed to be installed without using wax. They have a polystyrene cap, which should keep out stray fungus spores, but I use wax anyway, as some caps fall off. This type of spawn is a little less expensive and is said to produce mushrooms sooner.

Once you have inoculated the logs, store them in a place outside that doesn't get sun and is protected from wind. Lean the logs against a tree, putting scraps of lumber underneath to keep the logs out of the soil. You can also stack them like a miniature log cabin if you prefer, but start with untreated logs on the ground level. The logs shouldn't be allowed to dry out, so if it doesn't rain for a long time, water them, or even float them in your pond if you have one. The bathtub would work fine, too, I suppose. Unfortunately, you will have to wait for six months or a year for your first harvest.

Growing shiitakes is similar to fishing or playing cards. You never know when you will get lucky. I've had my largest harvests in spring and fall, but you never know when they will appear, nor how many. You can't plan a dinner party and depend on them for the menu. But that's part of what makes them so special.

EATING SHIITAKE MUSHROOMS

Shiitakes are great eating, well worth the long months of waiting. Shiitake mushrooms have a unique flavor, unlike any other mushrooms I have eaten. You can sauté them in butter or add them to an omelet. No matter how you prepare them, begin by removing the stems, then tearing (not cutting) them into bite-size pieces. Discard the stems, which are very tough, or use them in soup stock. If you want to get fancier, try the recipe for Tuscan-Style Shiitake Mushrooms on this page, one of my favorites.

SQUASH
Cucurbita species
ANNE RAVER

If I could only take one vegetable to a desert island, it would not be squash. I do not feel the same passion for squash that I feel for, say, tomatoes (which would be my choice for the desert island), but my garden would seem empty without it. My vegetable patch would lack a certain boisterous charm without those tendrils reaching out beyond the fence, developing little suggestive bulbs that swell into baseball bats overnight; or scrambling up a fence and over an arbor, to dangle their fruits in visitors' faces. Winter squash also makes a colorful summer groundcover and can be planted on a slope. Doing so helps prevent erosion and gives those squash vines plenty of room to grow.

Squashes are American natives that have been cultivated for thousands of years. They were domesticated in Mexico and South America, which explains why they like to keep their feet warm. Summer squash, pumpkins, and acorn squash are all members of the same species, *Cucurbita pepo*. Other squash varieties, like 'Buttercup' and 'Golden Hubbard', belong to the species *C. maxima;* striped crookneck types, like the lovable 'Green Striped Cushaw', belong to *C. mixta;* and butternut varieties belong to *C. moschata*.

C. pepo is best picked tender and fresh. The *C. maxima* varieties will be sweeter if "cured" after harvesting for about ten days at 80°F to 85°F. *C. moschata* needs to cure about two months to be at its best. *C. mixta* should cure for at least ten days.

GROWING SQUASH

Squash is not a plant for a small garden, unless you grow a bush type bred not to sprawl, such as 'Jersey Golden', or train a vining type on a trellis, which is a lovely idea, because the flowers are wonderful to behold, swarming with bees. Squash needs rich, friable soil, so dig in plenty of compost and aged manure. Cucurbits do not like acid soil; they grow best when the pH is about 7 or higher. I plant the seeds directly in the soil after the weather warms up to about 80°F. In cooler climates, you can give plants a jump-start

Squashes, such as patty-pan above, have been cultivated in America for thousands of years.

93

by sowing seeds indoors two to three weeks before you intend to set out the seedlings. Plant two seeds to a four-inch pot; once they sprout, pinch off the weaker seedling. Transplant gently, as squash plants have taproots and do not cotton to being disturbed. But as the seeds germinate quickly and grow like gangbusters, it may not be necessary to give them a head start.

Basking in Maryland's warmth, I don't bother with any of this but sow my seeds in hills about five feet apart, with three to four seeds per hill. Then I just stand back and watch them grow. I give them plenty of water to keep them productive and tender.

One note of caution: *C. moschata* and *C. maxima* love to interbreed, so don't plant varieties of both species unless you can separate them by about 200 feet. Squash is also subject to squash vine borers and a number of diseases, but I find it's better not to worry about them unless (notice I didn't say until) they show up. If you have good soil, rotate your crops, and grow resistant varieties, you may never see a borer. If you do, cut the vine off and see if you can find the caterpillars. Sometimes the plant will recover. If it doesn't, pull it out. Squash is so prolific, you don't have to weep when it flops. Of course, if you don't mind your garden looking like a hospital ward, you can use row covers, but then you have to lift them off to let the flowers cross-pollinate. It seems a terrible bother.

Almost all cucurbits have male and female flowers. The male flowers, which usually appear first, have clusters of fused anthers covered with pollen; the female flowers have a sticky stigma waiting for a pollen-covered bee to drop by. It's easy to tell the two apart, and as long as you leave a few male flowers, you can eat the rest, dipped in batter and fried tempura-style.

RECOMMENDED VARIETIES

SUMMER SQUASH
Days to maturity listed below are counted from the time of planting seed.

'RONDO DE NICE'—60 days; heirloom; round green zucchini; pick at one inch and sauté whole; good for stuffing a little bigger.

'STRIATA D'ITALIA'—50 days; bushy plant; cylindrical fruits with mottled light and dark green stripes; excellent flavor and texture.

'SUNBURST'—52 days; bright yellow patty-pan type; pick at teacup size.

'TROMBONCINO'—60 days; rambling zucchini with five-foot runners; slender, yellowish-green fruit should be harvested at ten inches or less. If left on the vine, will grow to six-inch-wide, three-foot-long baseball bats. Give it a sturdy trellis and watch it grow over the house.

'ZEPHYR'—54 days; straight-neck type; yellow with green tip; nutty and firm; harvest at four inches long.

WINTER SQUASH
'BUTTERCUP'—94 days, Burgess strain, four- to five-pound flattened turbans; dark green rinds with button ends; excellent flavor.

'GREEN-STRIPED CUSHAW'—110 days; bulb-shaped striped crookneck; can reach ten-pounds; vines resistant to squash borer; whitish-green skin with green stripes; light yellow sweet flesh good for pies and baking.

'PIENA DI NAPOLI'—110 days; butternut type; deep green fruits turn gray with gold flecks; can grow to 2½ feet long; flavorful yellow-orange flesh; stores well.

'CHA-CHA'—95 days; Buttercup/Kabocha type; four to five pounds; dark green skin and bright orange flesh; sweet, nutty taste; long storage.

'DELICATA'—100 days; cream-colored with dark green stripes; sweet orange flesh; stores well.

'LONG ISLAND CHEESE'—108 days; heirloom; six to ten pounds; smooth, tan, ribbed, reminiscent of a wheel of cheese; great for baking pies.

'SPAGHETTI SQUASH'—88 days; oblong, three to five pounds; smooth ivory skin turns yellow as it matures; spaghettilike flesh; bake, fork out the "spaghetti," and top with sauce!

EATING SQUASH

When picked small, summer squashes are delicious sautéed quickly in garlic and olive oil. My mother loves to cut them up with fresh tomato, onion, and okra. Ellen and Shepherd Ogden, of The Cook's Garden, in Londonderry, Vermont, have a wonderfully simple way of cooking the heirloom 'Rondo de Nice': Pick the little round squashes when they are one inch in diameter and sauté them with a pinch of savory. When they get to tennis-ball size, stuff them with onion, tomato, cheese, and bread crumbs.

SQUASH (OR PUMPKIN) SOUP

1 winter squash, ideally 8 inches high and just as wide

2 tbsp. softened butter

Salt and black pepper

1 medium onion

¼ cup long-grain rice

3½ cups chicken stock

Freshly grated nutmeg or ground cumin to garnish

6 slices bacon, cooked until crisp

3 tbsp. mozzarella, crumbled

Cut a lid from the stalk end of the squash and scoop out the seeds. Rub butter around the flesh inside and season with salt and pepper. Place the onion and rice inside. In a saucepan, bring the stock to a boil. Put the pumpkin or squash in a big roasting pan, pour the stock into the squash, and replace the lid. Bake for two hours at 375°F. Remove the squash from the oven, take off lid, scrape some of the softened flesh from the walls into the soup and mix it in. Add either nutmeg or cumin, and season to taste. Garnish with bacon and mozzarella and serve. Serves four. (As a bonus, you get roasted seeds: Spread seeds on a baking sheet, sprinkle with salt, and bake at 375°F for 20 minutes.)

This recipe is adapted from *The New Kitchen Garden,* by Anna Pavord (Dorling Kindersley, 1996).

ZUCCHINI
'Costata Romanesca'
JOAN DYE GUSSOW

Until I grew *Cucurbita pepo* 'Costata Romanesca' (about which my seed catalog remarks, "This is the only zucchini to grow unless you like water"), my
yearly love affair with zucchini was always brief. Sometime in late May or
early June, when the danger of frost was reliably past in our New York garden, my husband, Alan, would pick a bed where we had not planted zucchini
in several years, deeply dig two or three circles, maybe a foot and a half in
diameter and six inches apart, and fork in manure and compost and a small
handful of bonemeal-bloodmeal-greensand mix. Then he would space three
or four half-finger-deep holes around the perimeter, two or three inches in
from the edge of the circle; drop a couple of seeds in each; fill the holes with
soil rubbed between his hands to make it fine; and water down the area.

Some days later—depending on the temperature—the hulking seedlings
would shoulder their way to the surface, first pushing their humped stems
out of the ground, then straightening up to wrench their giant seed leaves out
of the soil and up to the sun. Usually all of them came up, 2 from a hole, 8
from a circle, 24 in the bed. Then I would begin the battle to make Alan pull
most of them out to leave room for the giant plants they would become.
Usually he objected and left several more plants than we needed, but that
never stopped us from having zucchini. The first flowers were always the use-
less males, lots of them. I intend no social commentary here, just a statement
of the fact that until the emergence of a flower bud whose bulge where it
meets its stem shows it to be female, the male flowers are, from the stand-
point of a squash eater, pointless. I willingly acknowledge here that their
deeper purpose may be to inform a crowd of bees that pollen is available on
this site, so that when the female flowers open, there will be a glut of pollina-
tors. And of course, the males can be battered and fried, but if you're waiting
for zucchini, those boy flowers don't count.

Finally, a female bud emerges, enlarges, and opens. And quicker than you
expect, a slender green squash awaits your morning walk. But only briefly.
Go away for a weekend, or stay inside for a day or two of rain, and the petite
and tender squash has swelled up into a squash as big as your forearm. A day
or two later, there's nothing to be done but cut the monster from the vine and
sneak it into someone's unlocked car. And a few weeks later, of course, the
plants collapse, victims of squash vine borers.

But my worst problem with zucchini has never been its tendency to bloat
or die. It is that all the good recipes I have say, "Brown the slices," and that's
simply ridiculous. Put slices of your ordinary zucchini in a frying pan with
olive oil, and their pores open, spilling out enough water to eliminate any possibility of browning. It was many years before I discovered a technique for

Large and tasty, 'Costata Romanesca' contains much less water than other zucchini varieties, making it ideal for summer cooking.

browning zucchini that worked—you cut it into julienne strips. The channels that carry fluid from the base of the fruit to its tip run up and down, so I'm guessing that when you cut them across, all the water leaks out, but when you cut them vertically, only the little cut ends leak. Voilà! Browning.

The other solution is 'Costata Romanesca', which you can cut up any way you like. My next-door community gardeners love the fruits but won't grow them because the plants are so huge that they each take up half of a nine- by ten-foot plot. Gigantism allows them to tough out the unfailing borer attack. Not only that, the fruits are beautiful—dark and light green, heavily ribbed, and slightly twisted. And when they get big, even really big, you can still use them. Indeed, you can leave one on the kitchen counter for a week and it won't get soft or spoil, and when you cut it, it will still be tender from the skin in. If you are fortunate and have a garden big enough to grow these gentle giants, you will discover that the catalog is right. 'Costata Romanesca' can be sliced, cubed, or even shredded without presenting you with a pan of water. And when you arrive for dinner carrying a two-pound fruit, everyone will smile.

TOMATOES
Lycopersicum esculentum
LEE REICH

Some people, many of them gardeners, believe that the secret to eating a delectable tomato is to grow it yourself. Second best, they say, is farm-fresh. At the risk of committing horticultural sacrilege, I say "not so" in both cases.

Ripeness is, of course, important to great flavor; an unripe tomato tastes no better than cotton soaked in diluted lemon juice. But if truth be told, tomatoes picked slightly underripe can still ripen to perfection off the plant, as do bananas, winter apples, and pears. (Not every fruit ripens after picking.)

The real secret to eating a delectable tomato is to find a variety that was selected for its great taste. There are hundreds and hundreds of tomato varieties around, but many have been selected or bred for commercially desirable qualities such as high yield, good appearance, or a concentrated ripening period. Other varieties are notable for disease resistance or early availability.

My first consideration in choosing a tomato variety is flavor. Highly touted resistance to "VFN" does not impress me because *Verticillium* wilt, *Fusarium* wilt, or nematodes, which VFN denotes, never rear their heads in my garden, nor in many other gardens. Likewise, I'll generally not shy away from a good-tasting variety that is low-yielding, because I can compensate by putting in a few extra plants. And while it's true that the convolutions that catface my 'Belgian Giant' tomato make the fruits ugly, their rich flavor more than compensates for the lack of beauty.

As a sweeping generalization, so-called "indeterminate" tomato varieties taste best. These are varieties that form fruits along their ever-elongating stems. In contrast, the fruits of "determinate" varieties terminate a stem, so further growth is from side branches, which in turn are terminated by fruits. Because of the way they grow, determinate varieties produce fruits earlier and have a concentrated ripening period. However, indeterminate varieties taste much better because they have a higher ratio of leaves to fruits. I'd rather wait a little longer for my first tomatoes than eat an insipid 'Sub-Arctic Cherry' or 'Roma' tomato, both of which are determinate. Seed packets and nursery catalogs list the category in which a variety belongs.

GROWING TOMATOES

Starting your own tomato plants from seed is not at all difficult—and usually it is a necessity when you want to grow special varieties, named or otherwise. Sow seeds indoors about seven weeks before the expected date of the last spring frost in your area, keeping the growing seedlings on the cool side and in bright light. Around the last frost date, take them outside for a few hours each day to gradually acclimatize them to sun, wind, and even cooler temperatures. A week or so later, plant them out in the garden. The ideal location is a spot that receives at least six hours of direct sunlight each day and is as far away as possible from the area where you planted tomatoes in the past two years.

When you start tomato plants from seed, you can choose from an abundance of tasty heirloom varieties, such as those shown above.

A sprawling tomato plant takes up lots of space and bears a messy, sprawling load of fruit. A staked tomato plant takes up less space and yields cleaner and earlier fruit. Because staked plants can stand 18 inches apart and grow upward, they yield more from a given area of ground than sprawling plants. Only indeterminate varieties are suitable for staking. I plant two rows down a 36-inch-wide bed, then stake and ruthlessly prune each plant to a single, main stem. Side shoots develop wherever a leaf joins the stem. I go through my tomato bed at least weekly, pulling off side shoots and also tying the main stems to their stakes.

To sleuth out those tomatoes best suited for your taste buds, listen to other gardeners' opinions, read about tomatoes, and try out as many as you can next summer. If you fall in love with what you're sinking your teeth into, order seeds for the following season. Can't find out what they're called? No need to forsake the best tomatoes just because you can't put a name on them. Many great-tasting tomatoes are nonhybrid or heirloom varieties, which means you can save their seeds and plant them the following year! The seeds of hybrids usually do not "come true," or produce the same variety; they may revert back to traits of parents that were used to breed them. Sometimes wily seed sellers will call a variety a hybrid just to discourage seed saving, so if you suspect that's the case, give it a whirl.

Saving tomato seeds entails nothing more elaborate than squeezing a bit of the seed-gel mix out of the cavity of a tomato fruit into a glass. (No need even to sacrifice the whole tomato, you can eat the rest of the fruit.) The seed gel contains inhibitors that keep the seeds from sprouting while they're still

Paste tomatoes are destined for the pot. Above is 'San Marzano', sweet and richly flavored when cooked, but mealy and flavorless raw.

inside the fruit, but it's easy to leach and ferment these inhibitors away by adding some water to the seed-gel mix. After letting the slurry sit for a day or so, pour it through a fine strainer, wash the seeds well in running water, and spread them out to dry. Pack the dried seeds in sealed containers kept in a cool location.

RECOMMENDED VARIETIES

TOMATOES BEST EATEN FRESH

'BELGIAN GIANT'—85 days; indeterminate; large, dark pink fruit; sweet, mild, excellent flavor.

'BRANDYWINE'—95 days; indeterminate; large, firm, rosy light pink fruit; excellent flavor.

'VALENCIA'—75 days; indeterminate; medium-size smooth and round orange fruit; good flavor.

'GARDENER'S DELIGHT'—65 days; indeterminate cherry tomato; large plant; red fruit; midseason; sweet and tangy; good productivity.

'SUN CHERRY'—58 days; indeterminate cherry tomato; large plant; red fruit; midseason; sweet and tangy; good productivity.

'SUN GOLD'—57 days; indeterminate cherry tomato; large plant; orange fruit; early season; sweet and tangy; good productivity.

'SWEET MILLION'—65 days; indeterminate cherry tomato; large plant; red fruit, midseason; sweet and tangy; average productivity.

'Sun Gold' is a sweet and tangy cherry tomato that ripens early, a harbinger of things to come later in the season when larger varieties are ready for harvest.

TOMATOES SUITABLE FOR COOKING AND CANNING

'AMISH PASTE'—85 days; indeterminate paste tomato; poor texture and flavor raw; full-bodied and rich-tasting cooked.

'ANNA RUSSIAN'—70 days; indeterminate paste tomato; juicy with mild good flavor fresh; very tomato-ey and sweet with a slight tang cooked.

'HOWARD'S GERMAN'—80 days; indeterminate paste tomato; somewhat tangy and smooth, very good raw; sweet and tangy and richly flavored cooked.

'SAN MARZANO'—77 days; indeterminate paste tomato; flavorless, dry, and mealy fresh, sweet and richly flavored cooked.

Days to maturity are counted from the time of transplanting.

EATING TOMATOES

Juicy slices of succulent raw tomato bring the dullest sandwich to life. I thoroughly enjoy 'Belgian Giant' in a sandwich of homemade bread topped with fresh basil ('Sweet' or 'Fino Verde') along with chopped green onions, lettuce, and perhaps a small dab of mustard. Coarsely chopped or sliced, tomatoes take center stage in a salad accompanied by plenty of fresh basil and drizzled with olive oil and red wine vinegar. They also pair nicely with cooked beans or grains and fresh herbs for a quick, nutritious summer meal. And the possibilities for cooking with tomatoes are, of course, legend. Just remember to grow enough paste tomatoes to have some of summer's bounty left over for freezing or canning to carry you through the long tomato-less months.

646-5

USDA HARDINESS ZONE MAP

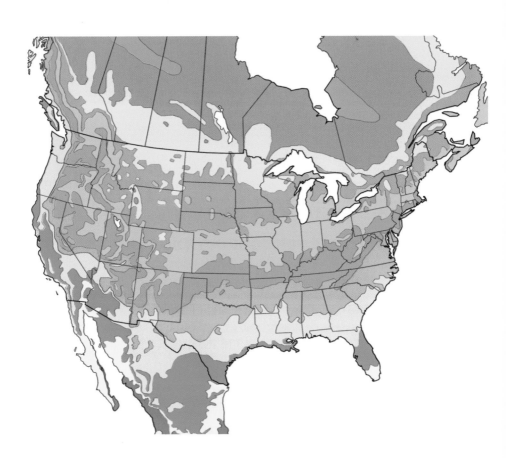

ZONES & MINIMUM WINTER TEMPERATURES (°F.)

Zone 1 below –50°	**Zone 5** –20° to 10°	**Zone 9** 20° to 30°
Zone 2 –50° to –40°	**Zone 6** –10° to 0°	**Zone 10** 30° to 40°
Zone 3 –40° to –30°	**Zone 7** 0° to 10°	**Zone 11** above 40°
Zone 4 –30° to –20°	**Zone 8** 10° to 20°	

FOR MORE INFORMATION

SEED TO SEED: SEED SAVING TECHNIQUES FOR THE VEGETABLE GARDENER
Suzanne Ashworth
Seed Savers Exchange/Chelsea Green, 1991

THE NEW SEED-STARTER'S HANDBOOK
Nancy Bubel
Rodale, 1988

THE NEW ORGANIC GROWER'S FOUR-SEASON HARVEST: HOW TO HARVEST FRESH, ORGANIC VEGETABLES FROM YOUR HOME GARDEN ALL YEAR LONG
Eliot Coleman
Chelsea Green, 1992

THE WINTER HARVEST MANUAL
Eliot Coleman; 1998
Four Season Farm, 609 Weir Cove Road, Harborside, ME 04642

THE EDIBLE GARDEN SERIES
(ten volumes)
Rosalind Creasy
Tuttle/Periplus, 1999–2000

LIVING SEASONALLY: THE KITCHEN GARDEN AND THE TABLE AT NORTH HILL
Joe Eck and Wayne Winterrowd
Henry Holt, 1999

THIS ORGANIC LIFE: CONFESSIONS OF A SUBURBAN HOMESTEADER
Joan Dye Gussow
Chelsea Green, 2001

STRAIGHT-AHEAD ORGANIC: A STEP-BY-STEP GUIDE TO GROWING GREAT VEGETABLES IN A LESS-THAN-PERFECT WORLD
Shepherd Ogden
Chelsea Green, 1999

CREATIVE VEGETABLE GARDENING: ACCENTING YOUR VEGETABLES WITH FLOWERS
Joy Larkcom
Abbeville, 1997

COMING HOME TO EAT: THE PLEASURES AND POLITICS OF LOCAL FOODS
Gary Paul Nabhan
W.W. Norton, 2001

THE GARDENER'S TABLE: A GUIDE TO NATURAL VEGETABLE GROWING AND COOKING
Richard Merrill and Joe Ortiz
Ten Speed Press, 2000

THE HARROWSMITH COUNTRY LIFE BOOK OF GARDEN SECRETS
Dorothy Hinshaw Patent and Diane E. Bilderback
Camden House, 1991

THE PRACTICAL GARDENER: A GUIDE TO BREAKING NEW GROUND
Roger B. Swain
Little Brown, 1989; Galahad, 1997

100 VEGETABLES AND WHERE THEY CAME FROM
William Woys Weaver
Algonquin, 2000

HEIRLOOM VEGETABLE GARDENING
William Woys Weaver
Henry Holt, 1997

SEED SAVERS EXCHANGE: THE FIRST TEN YEARS
Kent Whealy and Arllys Adelmann
Seed Saver Publications, 1986
Also three annual publications sent to members: *Seed Savers Yearbook, Seed Savers Summer Edition,* and *Seed Savers Harvest Edition* (www.seedsavers.org)

SEED SOURCES

ABUNDANT LIFE SEED FOUNDATION
P.O. Box 772
Port Townsend, WA 98368
360-385-5660; 360-385-7455 fax
www.abundantlifeseed.org

BAKER CREEK HEIRLOOM SEEDS
2278 Baker Creek Road
Mansfield, MO 65704
417-924-8917 (also fax)
www.rareseeds.com

BOUNTIFUL GARDENS
18001 Shafer Ranch Road
Willits, CA 95490
707-459-6410; 707-459-1925 fax
www.bountifulgardens.org

W. ATLEE BURPEE & CO.
300 Park Avenue
Warminster, PA 18974
800-888-1447; 800-487-5530 fax
www.burpee.com

THE COOK'S GARDEN
P.O. Box 535
Londonderry, VT 05148
800-457-9703
www.cooksgarden.com

EASTERN NATIVE SEED CONSERVANCY
P.O. Box 451
Great Barrington, MA 01230
413-229-8316
http://gemini.berkshire.net/ensc/

FEDCO SEEDS
P.O. Box 520-A
Waterville, ME 04903
207-872-8317 fax
www.fedcoseeds.com

HARDSCRABBLE ENTERPRISES INC.
P.O. Box 1124
Franklin, WV 26807
304-358-2921 (also fax)
(Shiitake spawn)

HEIRLOOM GARDENS
13889 Dupree Worthey Road
Harvest, AL 35749
256-233-4422
www.heirloomnursery.com

HEIRLOOM SEEDS
P.O. 245
West Elizabeth, PA 15088
412-384-0852
www.heirloomseeds.com

HIGH MOWING SEEDS
813 Brook Road
Wolcott, VT 05680
802-888-1800; 802-888-8446 fax
www.highmowingseeds.com

J.L. HUDSON, SEEDSMAN
Star Route 2, Box 337
La Honda, California 94020
www.jlhudsonseeds.net
(Ethnobotanical catalog of seeds)

IRISH EYES—GARDEN CITY SEEDS
P.O. Box 307
Thorp, WA 98946
509-964-7000; 800-964-9210 fax
www.irish-eyes.com

JOHNNY'S SELECTED SEEDS
184 Foss Hill Road
Albion, ME 04910
207-437-9294; 800-437-4290 fax
www.johnnyseeds.com

MOOSE TUBERS
For address see Fedco Seeds, above
(Seed potatoes)

MUSHROOM HARVEST
P.O. Box 5727
Athens, OH 45701
740-448-6105; 740-448-8007 fax
(Shiitake spawn)

NATIVE SEEDS/SEARCH
526 North Fourth Avenue
Tucson, AZ 85705
520-622-5561; 520-622-5591 fax
www.nativeseeds.org

NICHOLS GARDEN NURSERY
1190 Old Salem Road NE
Albany, OR 97321
800-422-3985; 800-231-5306 fax
www.nicholsgardennursery.com

REDWOOD CITY SEED COMPANY
P.O. Box 361
Redwood City, CA 94064
650-325-7333
www.batnet.com/rwc-seed

RENEE'S GARDEN SEEDS
7389 West Zayante Road
Felton, CA 95018
888-880-7228; 831-335-7227 fax
www.reneesgarden.com   .

SEED SAVERS EXCHANGE
3076 North Winn Road
Decorah, IA 52101
563-382-5990; 563-382-5872 fax
www.seedsavers.org

SEEDS OF CHANGE
P.O. Box 15700
Santa Fe, NM 87506
888-762-7333
www.seedsofchange.com

SHEPHERD'S GARDEN SEEDS
30 Irene Street
Torrington, CT 06790
860-482-3638
www.shepherdseeds.com

SOUTHERN EXPOSURE SEED EXCHANGE
P.O. Box 460
Mineral, VA 23117
540-894-9480; 540-894-9481 fax
www.southernexposure.com

TERRITORIAL SEED COMPANY
P.O. Box 158
Cottage Grove, OR 97424
541-942-9547; 888-657-3131 fax
www.territorial-seed.com

THOMAS JEFFERSON CENTER FOR HISTORIC PLANTS
Monticello
P.O. Box 316
Charlottesville, VA 22902
434-984-9821
www.monticello.org/shop

UNDERWOOD GARDENS
1414 Zimmerman Road
Woodstock, IL 60098
888-382-7041 fax
www.underwoodgardens.com

CONTRIBUTORS

SUSAN BELSINGER is a culinary educator, food writer, and photographer. Her work frequently appears in national magazines and newspapers, and she has co-authored more than a dozen books, including several best-selling, award-winning cookbooks. Besides gardening at her home in Brookeville, Maryland, she lectures frequently on herbs, edible flowers, chiles, garlic, healthy cuisine, cooking with kids, and aromatherapy.

ELIZABETH BURGER is a sculptor in multimedia, currently harvesting pond algae, water hyacinth roots, okra roots, seedpods, bird's nests, and willow for her various creations. Working in her studio in Maryland in a barn overlooking five acres, which include a stream, a pond, and the garden where okra is treated like royalty, she teaches art at local colleges and runs workshops on her land.

ELIOT COLEMAN is the author of *Four Season Harvest* (Chelsea Green, 1992), *The New Organic Grower* (Chelsea Green, 1995), and the self-published *Winter Harvest Manual* (1998). **BARBARA DAMROSCH** is the author of *The Garden Primer* (Workman, 1988) and *Theme Gardens* (Workman, newly revised 2001). Together they operate Four Season Farm, a commercial market garden in Harborside, Maine.

ROSALIND CREASY is a writer, photographer, and landscape designer with a passion for beautiful vegetables and ecologically sensitive gardening. Her 1982 bestseller, *The Complete Book of Edible Landscaping* (Sierra Club Books) is still used in college courses, and her 1988 *Cooking From the Garden* (Sierra Club Books), though out of print, is a bible for regional cooks. She is a regular contributor to *The Los Angeles Times, Garden Design,* and *Country Living Gardener.* Her *Edible Garden Series* (Tuttle/Periplus, 1999–2000) won a Quill and Trowel Award from the Garden Writers Association of America in 2001.

JOAN DYE GUSSOW is a longtime organic gardener as well as Mary Swartz Rose Professor Emerita and former chair of the Nutrition Education Program at Teachers College, Columbia University. Currently chair of the board of Just Food and a member of the Chefs' Collaborative Board of Overseers, she has published a variety of books and articles. Her most recent book, *This Organic Life: Confessions of a Suburban Homesteader,* was published in June 2001 by Chelsea Green.

HENRY N. HOMEYER is a lifelong organic gardener, a garden designer, and the author of *Notes From the Garden: Reflections and Observations of an Organic Gardener* (University Press of New England, 2002). He gardens by a winding stream at his home in Cornish Flat, New Hampshire, and his weekly gardening column appears in a dozen newspapers around New England as well as on his web site, www.gardening-guy.com. He is the Vermont–New Hampshire editor of *People, Places, and Plants* magazine and a regular contributor to National Public Radio.

JOAN JACKSON was garden editor for *The San Jose Mercury News,* in California, and a columnist for Knight-Ridder News Service for 25 years. Now retired, she writes articles on gardening for California newspapers. She lives in northern California with her husband, Wally, an expert vegetable gardener. Her main interests are vegetables, native plants, and sustainable gardening. In her spare time she grows a backyard full of gourds, with the help of her grandson, Keith.

GARY PAUL NABHAN is director of the Center for Sustainable Environments at Northern Arizona University and author of 14 books, most recently, *Coming Home to Eat: The Pleasures and Politics of Local Foods* (W.W. Norton, 2001). A recipient of the MacArthur Foundation Genius Award, Nabhan cofounded Native Seeds/SEARCH. At the moment, he raises Navajo-Churro sheep and native vegetable crops adapted to semidesert climates at his home near Winona, Arizona.

ELLEN OGDEN is cofounder of The Cook's Garden seed catalog, based in Londonderry, Vermont, specializing in herbs and salad greens since 1980. She writes about food and cooking from the garden. Her new book, *The Cook's Garden,* will be published by William Morrow in spring 2003.

ANNE RAVER writes about gardening, nature, and the environment for *The New York Times*. She is the author of *Deep in the Green: An Exploration of Country Pleasures* (Knopf, 1995) and is at work on another book about returning to her family farm in Maryland. She frequently lectures about her travels and efforts to preserve the rural and natural environment in a world of golf courses and malls. A former Loeb Fellow at Harvard University's Graduate School of Design, she is the recipient of the American Horticultural Society's 2002 Horticultural Writing Award.

LEE REICH is a garden writer, consultant, and avid gardener who has worked in soil and plant research for the USDA and Cornell University. His books include *Uncommon Fruits Worthy of Attention* (Addison Wesley Longman, 1991), *A Northeast Gardener's Year* (Perseus, 1992), *The Pruning Book* (Taunton Press, 1997), and *Weedless Gardening* (Workman, 2001). His articles have appeared in *Fine Gardening, Organic Gardening,* and *The New York Times;* his gardening column for Associated Press appears weekly in newspapers across the country.

CAROLE SAVILLE is a food and garden writer and author of *Exotic Herbs* (Henry Holt, 1997) as well as contributing editor to *Country Living Gardener*. She lives and gardens in the San Francisco Bay area.

RENEE SHEPHERD has made a career of introducing international specialty vegetables, flowers, and herbs to home gardeners. Her seed company, Renee's Garden, based in Felton, California, offers seed packets through independent garden centers nationwide or on the Internet. She speaks to many gardening groups and writes for gardening and cooking periodicals. She is currently completing her third cookbook.

LYNETTE L. WALTHER, a former college educator, is the recipient of the National Garden Bureau's Exemplary Journalism Award and the Florida Magazine Association's Silver Award of Writing Excellence. She is the author of two books and currently writes a gardening column for *The Palatka Daily News* and regional magazines in Florida. She divides her gardening time between northeast Florida and mid-coast Maine.

PHOTOS

DAVID CAVAGNARO cover, pages 1, 4, 6, 8 top, 9, 12, 14, 15, 16, 18, 23, 28, 31, 32, 36, 37, 38, 39, 41, 42, 46, 49, 53, 56, 58, 61, 62, 64, 66, 67, 68, 74, 77, 79, 80, 84, 85, 86, 88, 90, 97, 99, 100
NEIL SODERSTROM pages 7, 8 bottom
BARBARA DAMROSCH pages 10, 11, 13, 87
ROSALIND CREASY pages 20, 21
DEREK FELL pages 25, 27, 73, 93
JERRY PAVIA pages 34, 35, 47, 76, 83
ALAN & LINDA DETRICK pages 65, 70, 101

INDEX

BROOKLYN BOTANIC GARDEN

World renowned for pioneering gardening information, Brooklyn Botanic Garden's 21st-Century Gardening Series of award-winning guides provides spectacularly photographed, compact, practical advice for gardeners in every region of North America.

To order other fine titles published by BBG, call 718-623-7286, or shop in our online store at www.bbg.org/gardenemporium. For more information on Brooklyn Botanic Garden, including an online tour, visit www.bbg.org or call 718-623-7200.

MORE BOOKS ON KITCHEN GARDENING